COOK
like a Mother!
CLEAN
like a Pro!

COOK

like a Mother!

CLEAN

like a Pro!

THE SINGLE DAD'S GUIDE TO COOKING AND CLEANING

BY

PETER WRIGHT

2002 TORONTO, CANADA

Ordering information:
Distributed in Canada by Hushion House Publishing Ltd.
36 Northline Road Toronto, Ontario Canada M4B 3E2
Phone (416) 285-6100, Fax (416) 285-1777

National Library of Canada Cataloguing in Publication
Wright, Peter, 1956-
    Cook like a mother! Clean like a pro! :
    the single dad's guide to cooking and cleaning / by Peter Wright.

Includes index.
ISBN 0-9689462-0-8

1. Cookery. 2. House cleaning. 3. Single fathers. I. Title.
TX652.W79 2002   641.5'12   C2002-901727-0

Cover / book design:	Karen Petherick,
	Intuitive Design International Ltd., Markham, Ontario
Illustrations:	Michael Petherick and Colleen Lynch
Cover Photo:	Helen Tansey Photography

Printed and bound in Canada

The following product and company names appearing in the book are trademarks or trade names of their respective companies: T-Fal Clipso, Iron, Proctor and Gamble Wetjet Swiffer, Swiffer, Reckitt Benckiser Antibacterial Spray/Wipes, Pillsbury One Step Cookies/Brownies/Crescent Rolls, Nabisco Chips Ahoy, Nestlé, Supertek Micro Fiber Cloths, Pizza Pops, Pam cooking spray, Kraft Macaroni and Cheese (Dinner), Minute Rice, Hamburger Helper, Lipton, Kellogg's Pop Tarts, Chef Boy R Dee, Bailey's Irish Cream, Grand Marnier, Showtime Rotisserie, Nintendo, Ziploc Containers and Sandwich Bags, Black and Decker Mini Chopper, Jell-o, Classico Pasta Sauces, Worcestershire Sauce, Bovril, Oxo Cube, Knorr, Aunt Jemima, Mattel Barbie, Fruit Loops, Dijon Mustard, Kellogg's Rice Krispies, Mr. Christie's Wafers, Quaker Oats, Smarties, Sara Lee Cheesecake, Tide.

Disclaimer: Although recipes have been tested, the author does not assume any responsibility for errors.

This book is dedicated to
the two most cherished people in my life:
Spencer and Taylor

CONTENTS

FOREWORD

Very few of us who get married expect to be single again. In our single twenties, it was sort of a rite of passage to eat fast food and not spend much time in the kitchen. Once we've been married, however, and we're used to eating substantially better than we did in our single days, it's difficult to redevelop a taste for fast food and lousy meals – to say nothing, of course, of having to feed your kids regardless of what your custody arrangements are. When I first began writing this book, my goal was to write down the recipes and housekeeping tricks that have kept my kids well fed and my house functionally clean. There was so much I had to learn. I've had to ask cooking questions of my mother, my sisters, mothers of kids I coach, store clerks – anyone who might have known the answer. Questions like, "How many minutes per pound does a whole chicken take to cook in the oven?" "Do I have to add liquid?" "How long can I keep a jar of pasta sauce in the fridge?" "What about leftovers?"

I have had to ask questions that I'm certain are the male equivalent of asking which direction – clockwise or counter-clockwise – tightens a bolt or screw. Thus, the info in the section, Stuff Worth Knowing, is so you won't have to suffer the impatient sighs these questions usually generated. But I prevailed, largely, if not exclusively, out of the need to feed my children and myself something that was tasty, FAST and presumably wouldn't make us ill. And, if truth be known, to have the satisfaction of doing it myself.

The many facets of *Cook Like A Mother! Clean Like a Pro!* are aimed primarily at the guy who grew up with a stay-at-home mom. Stuff to Make deals with the meals, Stuff to Make it With deals with making sure you have what you need to make your meals. Stuff to Make It In deals with having the stuff that I think is the easiest and fastest stuff to make your meals in. Stuff to Clean it Up With deals with the products that clean things easiest and fastest. Stuff Worth Knowing deals with knowing what simple practices can avoid illnesses. And lastly, Stuff Your Kids Can Do deals with the benefits/approaches to chores and allowances. For the occasions you'd like to impress a first date with your cooking prowess, the section, The Good Stuff, provided by my nephew who happens to be a very good cook, has recipes that would never be confused with recipes from a mother. This section is, shall we say, for the more confident cooks.

Looking back, if your mom was like mine, she was there when you returned from school and she cooked virtually every single meal. The only time your father cooked was if your mother was away, and I'll bet the meal entailed either something barbecued, fried or arrived in an old, beat-up VW Bug. It is also a safe bet that your mother and sisters cleared the table, and your household responsibilities were limited. With this in mind, I faced a considerable challenge in writing down the recipes in this book. With most recipe books, they assume you know the basics. With *Cook Like A Mother!*, I'll assume you know next to nothing. That way, when you're a competent cook, you'll be able to fly by the hints, facts and tips that help the first few times you don the chef's hat.

As a single father, I've strived to minimize the differences between the life my kids had as part of a traditional family and their new life living with each parent separately. I wanted to maintain my previous level of physical activity with my kids – throwing the baseball and football around, playing road hockey, riding our bikes – just spending time together. I didn't want one of the most important elements of my kids' and my relationship to be compromised just because their mother and I no longer lived together.

In my new role as the primary cook, however, I was determined to make meals that were tasty, nutritious, comforting – and fast. I wanted to do my best to ensure the meals I made didn't make my kids miss their mother unnecessarily, something I was concerned would happen if my idea of meal experimentation meant using a different cheese in a grilled cheese sandwich. And as the sole parent, I also tried to follow routines we had when we were a family. Our family routine of, say, having pizza on Friday night, was maintained – religiously. If we all ate dinner together before, then it was important we continued eating together now, even if was only my two kids and me. Of course, the big challenge was learning to do everything, from cooking, making lunches, to cleaning up – regardless of whose job it was while still married.

Ultimately, I want to provide you with the tricks and tools to either pull your own weight in the arena of cooking and cleaning or learn to be self-sufficient so you won't have to rely on the first gal that comes along with a nice set of casserole dishes – and God knows how tempting that will be.

INTRODUCTION
(Or, When's Dinner!)

Let's think for a moment about growing up. Wasn't it great how your meals somehow appeared day after day and how good they were? What comes to mind when you conjure up these meals? Were they comforting? Tasty? Nutritionally balanced? The meals our mothers cooked had two things in common: a personal touch and a terrific texture. There was always something special Mom did in preparing meals or dishes that was unique, something that made her meatloaf, spaghetti sauce, lasagna, roast beef, pot roast, pancakes, chocolate chip cookies – you name it, special. They tasted great and they had great texture (except for vegetables, let's leave vegetables out of this: mothers universally overcook vegetables – it's a secret pact).

And if you're like every other guy growing up on this planet, when lunch or dinner was over, you ran out the door as you swallowed the last bite to resume playing with your friends. We were busy, games to play, cats to terrorize, girls to bug. Did we ever say, "Gee Mom, that meatloaf was great. How exactly did you make it – I'm a few minutes early for our ball game?" Sure. So, when it was time to leave Mom's home for school or work, off we went to conquer the world and to fend for ourselves in the cooking and cleaning arenas. Wasn't pretty, was it? We may have been *well fed* growing up but we certainly weren't *well trained* to cook or clean. Some guys went straight to marriage where wifey generally was fortunate enough to assume the role as primary cook. Which, of course, is fine – as long as Mrs. Newly Married never gets tired of cooking all the meals.

Of course, a key question remains: can a guy *Cook Like A Mother!?* Most of us guys are in a love-to-eat, don't-like-to-cook-or-clean quandary. So, are there tricks or products that we can use that can help us guys cook and clean easier? The good news: there are. And we're going to go through this learning stuff together, man-to-man. I'll increase your domestic IQ, and while you won't necessarily enjoy it, I won't tick you off, either. I'm going to pass on to you the guy's way of doing things. If the kitchen is a minefield, I'll arm you with the weapons and skills you need to stay alive and well fed – without having to rely on anyone, ever.

Lastly, I think it's important for us guys to overcome an innate fear of the unknown: cooking for us is like computers for seniors – we're always afraid we'll break the recipe. It's far simpler just to plead ignorance. We have to learn we're not going to break the recipe (maybe the stove because we keep turning on the wrong element, but not the meal); it may not taste as good as it might, but we won't break it. I'm aware that the recipes in this book are rather rudimentary, but that's the kind of cook I am. On the other hand, I can assure you the majority of the recipes are nutritionally well balanced – the chocolate pancakes notwithstanding.

There are roughly 30 recipes in *Cook Like A Mother!*, from stuff to make for a fast dinner, to what to make when you've got time to make a feast. The recipes have been chosen for their independence, shall we say, from the need for exact measurements (everything's in cups and ounces, there's a Metric Conversion Chart at the end of the book for those inclined). These are just guides, though; the biggest thing we guys have to overcome is our fear of making a mistake in the kitchen. For me, the biggest mistake (aside from undercooking fish or chicken) is waiting for someone else to make you a good meal. Knowing how to cook nutritious and tasty meals for yourself or those you love is something that will never stop paying dividends.

Peter Wright

STUFF
TO
MAKE
IT WITH

This won't come as a huge surprise to you, but boys and girls are different. For all our efforts to raise gender-neutral children, boys – *for the most part* – are more familiar with skateboards and wrenches, and girls – *for the most part* – are more familiar with measuring cups and goldfish. Don't shoot me if you think I'm being sexist: I've got two boys and my girlfriend has two girls, so I speak from empirical observation. Yes, there are exceptions, and I certainly don't mean to annoy someone by pointing out an arguable obvious. With this in mind, if you had to choose a household location where the difference between men and women is the most marked, where would it be – the bathroom? Good guess, but too obvious.

Aside from personal hygiene products, there really isn't a big difference between a man's bathroom and a woman's bathroom – from a product standpoint. I didn't mention and won't get into whether their bathrooms are similar from a cleanliness standpoint. No, the room that single-handedly distinguishes men from women is the kitchen. Why? Because most guys don't know what's important to have on hand (we might not care, but for the sake of this book, let's say we have a passing interest).

Most girls have baked a cake, made dinner, made cookies or something kitchen-related, it seems, by the time they're 10 years old. The first time most guys step into the kitchen with any sense of purpose (and wonder) is when they've left home for university or work. Boys, *for the most part*, have used tools to fix their bikes, build a ramp, etc., or if they're asked to give their dads a hand. Girls, again, for the most part, help their moms in the kitchen, invariably, since their moms – who certainly don't like the fact – are still responsible for the majority of cooking and cleaning (I keep saying for the most part to avoid hitting my head on that low-slung overhead banner: "Sexist!")

It's not a surprise, then, that when a guy leaves home, whether from his wife or his dear old momma, the kitchen is an under-serviced part of his new digs. Arguably, the biggest difference between men and women is in the way they set up and keep a kitchen. This is an area that needs to be addressed because, in much the same way we couldn't expect to be effective – let alone successful – as a handyman with an incomplete, out-dated and barely functioning set of tools, we certainly can't expect to be a reasonably competent dinner engineer if there are big gaps in our kitchen arsenal.

4 Peter Wright

Frankly, if there was a game show that rewarded contestants on knowing what was necessary to stock even a very modest kitchen, guys – or at least the guys I've known – wouldn't win enough for cab fare home. So, I'm going to suggest some products that must be in your cupboard, pantry, fridge and freezer. We're after products that are perfect for us: Quick in, Quick out. Products that allow for a quick kitchen assault, limited ground support and voila! The meals they produce actually taste good, and you know what the taste test is: get your kids to try them. If your kids are between 6 and 16, you'll get honest immediate feedback on your cooking skills. After 7 years of cooking for my kids and me, my goal is simple: make it good enough for seconds.

The following is a list of stuff that you can accumulate over time, or in one fell swoop. This list has been chosen not just to reflect personal preferences but because of the meal possibilities that exist.

Freezer

French Fries
Frozen vegetables
Frozen dinners (for you)
Pizza Pops
Ice cream
Frozen lasagna
Frozen shepherd's pie
Chicken Fingers
Sandwich bags of lean ground beef
(this book is about fast choices – taking 10 minutes to divide a big thing of ground beef into usable portions makes life much easier).

Fridge

Don't forget, we're after options here. Having the following things in your fridge at most times opens up tasty, fast, healthy OPTIONS.

Pillsbury Crescent Rolls
Broccoli
Carrots
Celery

Onions
Peppers (green, red)
Cheese
Yogurt
Hot dogs
Ketchup
Mustard
Relish

Spice Cupboard

I don't know about you, but the first few times I cooked spaghetti sauce, way back when, I didn't use any spices. I thought it was great, until a friend of mine, a far more sophisticated person than me, said this tastes bland (that really wasn't the word he used, but you get the gist) – you should add some spices. So, with that in mind, it ain't complete until you add the spices. And, further to that, when they say "to taste," that's exactly what you'll do. You may *love* dill, so drown your sauce in dill. Just don't invite me.

Olive oil (Extra virgin is considered the finest)
Any other of cooking oil, such as Corn, Safflower, Canola Oil
Oregano
Garlic salt
Coarse pepper (ground)
Seasoning salt
Lemon pepper
Soya sauce
Steak seasoning
Tin of Pam (It may seem unlikely now, but you will use this stuff)
Balsamic vinegar (This seems to be the vinegar of choice for most recipes
    as well as women who want to contribute to dinner by making a salad)

Food Cupboard

I know buying all this stuff seems like a pain, so try to do big grocery-shopping expeditions rather than many little ones. Or, if your city has one of those on-line grocery services, try it. The one I use charges about $6.00 for delivery and a minimum order of $60, but it's such a treat having someone else schlep your groceries to the door.

Kraft Macaroni and Cheese (Dinner) (Yes, there are times you legitimately can resort to this)

Pillsbury One-Step Cookies/Brownies

Crackers (Saltine)

Chocolate milk powder

Cookies

Snacks (Find out what your kids' favorite snacks are and stock up. If you're a kid, there's nothing worse, and I mean nothing, than a snack-free or snack-challenged house)

Instant (Minute) rice

Pasta sauces

Tomato sauce

Pasta, different shapes (Rigatoni, penne, bowtie, spaghetti)*

Cans of tuna

Hamburger Helper

Lipton Side Dishes

Flavored rices

Potatoes

Pop Tarts

Cereal (Kind of obvious, I know)

Canned soups

Lipton Soupworks

Chef Boy R Dee (If you have kids, you're allowed, but – and take my word on this – don't let a woman your own age see you eating it)

You may have noticed there's no mention of chips. That's because I really like chips and the only way I'm not going to eat them is if I don't buy them. Also, crackers are a good, lower-fat substitute everyone seems to get used to. For a treat, say, the Super Bowl, I'll buy chips.

* The reason for having so many different pastas is simple: kids have a higher than average tolerance for repeat meals, and the trick to avoid exhausting this tolerance is to give a repeat an original look – different pasta or using rice is the best way.

Liquor Cabinet

Have this stuff on hand in case one of the single soccer moms – or the referee if she's over 18 and you drive a Porsche – accepts your dinner invitation with no lead time.

Bailey's Irish Cream	Cognac
Good dry white wine	Grand Marnier

Lastly, it's important for you to know how to use existing information. By this I mean asking the right people. I know this could be a direction-asking reluctance thing, but get over it – I ask everybody questions. I ask the butcher to suggest cuts of meat for the meal I'm preparing; I ask them how to cook certain meats. Aside from raising my cooking confidence, asking questions of these people seems to make them feel good, too. I ask the grocery store checkout people (if they're either matronly or attractive – the matronly ones at least can provide the answers, the attractive ones at least have to talk to you, which, as a middle-aged single father, has terrific value) for advice on meal preparation.

The *Cook Like A Mother!* Directive: avoid asking girlfriends or wives – existing, ex, or upcoming, any questions about how to prepare the meal we're cooking. This is our chance to prove we're capable. There's nothing worse, from a self-reliant standpoint, than to be asking questions every 3 minutes. Why? Because you're flirting with the ever-dangerous "Oh, I might as well do it myself!" When you've elicited this response, your stock not only didn't rise, it took a hit. No, we want to be able to start and finish this project.

STUFF
TO
MAKE
IT IN

When I was still dating my wife-to-be, mother of my children and ultimately ex-wife-to-be, I took up sports that I could play by myself because of how often I got stood up by her. It gave me a chance to experience windsurfing, competitive cycling and golf. The *Cook Like A Mother!* point of all this is that us guys know this fact: sports are really an elaborate justification for getting the stuff the sport requires. And it's not just *getting* the stuff that counts, it's getting the *right* stuff, the best stuff we can afford. Take bicycles, for example. You'd swear today's bikes are designed and built by the Stealth Bomber team. You can get tri-bars, clip-in pedal systems, Camelbak hydration systems, One Click shifting, carbon fiber frames, and the coolest aerodynamic 3 spoke wheels. You've just spent $5,000, but if you can afford it, there's no question having the right tools will enhance your performance and enjoyment. I used to marvel at one of my ex-brothers-in-law who was a rep for a sporting manufacturer. His van was a veritable toy store of windsurfing sails, bike gears, handlebars, wheels, helmets, intricate performance-enhancing parts – you name it. It was enough to make a salaried sports enthusiast salivate. It will never cease to amaze me the money that is spent at a recreation level on sporting equipment – just to enhance the experience.

What's the connection between pedaling and pasta, you ask? I believe the desire for "purity of performance" can be carried over to a guy's kitchen. I'm not kidding. There's a certain irony in having a $4,000 bike and a $4 garage sale pot. Why? Because, as with golf, biking, windsurfing or rock-climbing, tennis and whatever, we all know the better the stuff, the better we'll be. There's no question we'll be better at whatever we're doing if we have better stuff. It will certainly be more enjoyable using the right stuff – usually because performance is increased. (I know, I know, you could be one of the truly gifted athletes who doesn't need good equipment to perform – I used to race on second-hand racing skis, which were still better than new second-rate skis). How does this apply to being able to *Cook Like A Mother!?* We're also after speed in cooking and cleaning.

We're after performance. We want the best this baby can deliver – even if the baby we're referring to is a pressure cooker. Things become so much quicker – in all senses of the word, from cooking to clean up – when you use the right device.

How you fare as a cook and cleaner in your house largely depends on your choice and deployment of tools.

Peter Wright

The following are the devices I want you to get – it doesn't matter whether you ask for them for Christmas, birthdays, whatever. Nine times out of 10, a man won't walk out of a marriage or a family home with anything of value, kitchen-device wise. You'll get the casserole dish with the crack. You'll end up with the cookware that hasn't seen its non-stick surface for years. You'll get the mixer with only one speed that smells like an old train set when you use it. So you have to start from scratch. There are two lists: one is the must have, one is the nice-to-have-but-really-can-do-without. I know this list represents a considerable amount of money, but they're well worth it, believe me.

Must Have	Nice to Have
Toaster oven	Mini chopper
Chinese wok	Casserole dish
Pressure cooker	Indoor grill
Microwave	Containers for leftovers
Cookware	
Rotisserie oven	
Roasting pan	
Meat thermometer	
Timer	
Knife set	
Utensils	
Can opener	
Cookie tray	
Cutting board	
Measuring cup (glass)	
Auto turn-off coffee maker	
Oven mitts	

Device Details and Deployment

Must have ...

Toaster Oven   ... Of course this an obvious, but it is so much a must. Toaster ovens can double for your big oven, especially when the kids are away. These babies can bake cookies and poach a salmon. They can also make toast, oddly enough.

Wok   ... You know why woks are the perfect cooking tool for guys? Clean up. All you need is one of those little whisk things you can get when you buy your wok, put the wok under running water, use the whisk to get rid of whatever you cooked, and dry. No detergent required. It's important to add that the Chinese wok can't be one of those imposters you get at a department store. It can't be one of those ones that have an electric base. It has to be one of those ones you buy in Chinatown, or if you don't have a Chinatown where you live, you must take a trip to a city that has a Chinatown. I've bought two woks in my life; one was when I was 20 years old, the next one was when I was in my mid-30's. The key thing is that you buy an authentic Chinese wok because, believe it or not, they work better and let you do what you're supposed to do with a wok: cook limited amounts of food for a limited amount of time for a maximum amount of taste. In case you didn't know, woks were created at a time when food and fuel were in limited supply. The challenge was to cook a small quantity of food as quickly as possible and still make it tasty, and unintentionally, healthy. When I was in university, I used to buy a small steak and some broccoli and carrots, which, with rice could generate 3 suppers. It was kind of a test to see how authentic I could get to original wokery; it had a terrific mystical impact on me – ok, so that's bullshit, but the wok was perfect for me as "a starving student."

Mysticism aside, I defy anyone to equal the taste of food prepared in a wok versus food prepared in a western fry pan, even if it is wok-shaped.

Pressure Cooker   ... People are always intrigued that I use a
pressure cooker. People always express concern the lid's
going to fly off and dent the ceiling. The one I use, the T-
Fal Clipso, is amazing. The lid locking mechanism and the
stainless steel pot make it a great, essential addition to
my kitchen ('course, I've only ever used the T-Fal cooker,
so I can only comment on it). Pressure-cooking sounds so
old-fashioned, something that mothers used to do 30
years ago and really haven't done since. Back then,
pressure cookers were used to achieve a certain taste.
The fact is, a pressure cooker takes a third less time than
cooking conventionally. A third less time! For example, a
three-pound chicken takes 1 hour and 1/2 to cook,
conventionally. In the pressure cooker, it takes 25
minutes, then you brown it for 15. And while it's browning,
you can cook potatoes and carrots in it in less than 10
minutes. You can steam broccoli in 3 minutes in the
microwave.

I can't profess to use one because of a grand quest for
old style cooking, although I love the taste. My reasons
for using a pressure cooker are very simple: I can cook
meals without a terrific amount of planning. Conventional
cooking stipulates that if you want to cook a pot roast,
you need at least 4 hours cooking time. I don't have the
brain cells to plan and start cooking 4 hours before a
meal, but I still want the taste. Pressure-cooking allows
me to be the planning putz that I am but still have the
meals I want. Which means, and this will become more
meaningful to you as time goes on, that you can walk in
the door after picking up the kids at their friends', the
baby-sitter's, the after school program, whatever, at 5:30
p.m., take 15 minutes to prepare a chicken, get it cooking
and be sitting down to eat a made-from-scratch meal that
has, and I mean it, the comforting tastes you associate
with ol' Mom, at 6:30, give or take a few minutes. It also
means you can have a game of touch football on a
Sunday afternoon, get home at 3:30, read the paper, wait
until the games come on and still have beef stew, a pot
roast or chicken in time for 6:00.

Without getting too far ahead of myself, that in a nutshell is what I'm striving to do: help you, a guy like me, cook a meal that you, your kids and anyone you can attract long enough to feed, will really enjoy. How? By doing a few little things. Like getting the kids to put those Pillsbury crescent rolls on a cookie sheet so those can be baking while the chicken is browning. Believe it not, it's these types of things that will enable you to *Cook Like A Mother!* The one tip on pressure-cooking: when the device is under full pressure, you'll notice how much and with what intensity the steam is coming out of the valve. If you leave the element on full, the steam comes out at a great rate. It's best to turn down the element so that the steam is coming out steadily, just not like a madman. You'll have to experiment with this; when I first got my Clipso, I thought I had to have Old Faithful coming out, a big geyser, and my first meals ended up with nearly no liquid in them after cooking. So, experiment with how low you can turn the element and still have the steam coming out steadily. I can turn the element on my stove down to about 6.5 to 7, or with some stoves, medium high.

Microwave Oven   ... I know having a microwave oven sounds like a no-brainer, but some guys may try to get along without a microwave oven. My mother and brother don't have one. When my kids and I visit either one of them, it's like going back to a different era, to an era that, quite simply, took more time to prepare and cook things, and limited choices. And what's the credo of *Cook Like A Mother!*? Make it tasty, make it fast, and clean it quick. Don't worry, I know that tasty and microwave ovens don't belong in the same sentence. Tasty food from a microwave oven is an oxymoron. But, the microwave oven allows us the precise military timing that our modern mother-like cooking requires. It allows us to defrost ground beef for spaghetti sauce in 4 minutes, it allows us to defrost a chicken breast for BBQing in 4 minutes, and it allows us to cook vegetables in the same 4 minutes. Four minutes means everyone eats at 6:15 instead of 6:45, and that half-hour means choices – time to help with homework, put in the laundry, check the mail, read the paper – choices. It's important to address this device, if only because not to would be a serious omission. This is the device you'll be cooking the Kraft Macaroni and Cheese (Dinner) in for the kids, thawing meat, cooking vegetables, warming leftovers, and so on. But, you knew that. What you may not have known is how integral the microwave oven is to our cooking, which, given the time constraints we're under, must be planned and executed with military precision.

Cookware   ... Most guys would be happy with cookware they find at a garage sale, or handed down from relatives or friends. Bad idea. First of all, any protective coating will be a distant memory. Which means not only will things taste a little crappier than they should, they'll stick, and then make it difficult to clean. Difficult to clean means takes more time than it has to, and that wavers from our credo: Make it tasty, make it quick, clean it fast. Second of all, every time you pick these relics out of the cupboard, you will be reminded of the fact you're a single Dad. Regardless if we're preparing even a simple meal like Kraft Macaroni and Cheese (Dinner) or Chef Boy R Dee Ravioli, it is much easier on the psyche and self-esteem to be using cookware that still has some structural integrity and is remotely attractive. It even impresses the gals far, far more than old, mismatched, chipped crappyware.

Rotisserie Oven   ... Have you seen the infomercials for Showtime Rotisserie Ovens? Well, in my never-ending quest for really tasty meals made really easily and quickly, I got one. It's unbelievable. The ability to season, pierce and place a chicken on the rotisserie, slide it in, put the timer on, and put some vegetables for steaming on the top gives this appliance top marks in our Make it Quick, Make it Tasty school of cooking. This way, you save the trip to the store every time you want the delicious flavor – and aroma – of rotisserie cooking (I know this is kind of obvious, but this sort of thing still amazes me).

Roasting Pan ... How the hell do you propose cooking like a Mother if you don't have a simple roasting pan with cover that costs maybe $10? Seriously, buy a bigger one than you think. Buy one – ask the sales people (one that looks like she's turned on an oven at some point in her life) to recommend one that could do up to a 20 lb turkey).

Meat thermometer ... A meat thermometer is to the novice cook what the computer undo command is to a computer neo-nerd. This lets you never have to worry about unwittingly harming yourself or your children by under-cooking something. Forget "wait until the juices turn clear from pink" for chicken or turkey. Forget wondering exactly how many pounds was that thing. Just jab the damn thing with your trusty meat thermometer. Of course, this assumes you're following some sort of time cooking per weight equation. But more on that later on.

Timer ... Suggesting a timer is more of an aside than something you actually have to go out and acquire, but using one is probably the biggest adjustment you'll have to make. DON'T assume you'll remember when to turn things or retrieve them from whatever hot spot you left them in. Don't forget: our driving force behind *Cook Like A Mother!* is making things easy and as foolproof as possible. Having to remember to the check the clock, etc., adds the one thing we're working hard to avoid: tension. There's another purpose for the timer. If you have more than one child and they're both the age that enjoys, no, needs to play Nintendo and you get tired of listening to them argue, the timer introduces an impartial marshal. Each has the same time to play and when the timer speaks, they must abide – or you get to store the Nintendo in the closet (or if it's more convenient, the bottom of a very large lake).

Knife Set ... One of the greatest pleasures a man can have (in the dining room) is being the carver for Thanksgiving or Christmas dinner. As the gleaming knife slices through the turkey you cooked to perfection, your girlfriend, kids, parents, cousins, stragglers and so on, look at you lovingly and with anticipation for their dinner. As you pass them plate after plate of finely sliced meat, they marvel at your skill as a carver and as a cook. All is right in the world with a sharp carving knife. Of course, a different scenario takes place if you don't have a sharp knife: you have the pleasure of shredding off pieces of meat so small they're perfect for the turkey casserole or sandwiches to follow. I think the best thing to do is either to request a knife set for a gift or go to a store that has knowledgeable staff and ask them to recommend a versatile knife set for the kind of stuff you'll be doing. Don't buy the cheapest set. There's a good reason they're cheap: the metal doesn't hold an edge or can't achieve an edge. I have one of those sets that come in a wooden block. I like it because they're handy and you don't have to root through your drawers with greasy hands looking for the right knife. A good set should include a bread knife, a couple of paring knives, a honking cleaver for those reluctant chicken parts (I have to admit, I don't use the cleaver very often but every so often it's great to come crashing down on a piece of meat), and a couple of full-bladed knives.

Utensils   ... I know, utensils sound terrifically girly. Allen keys aren't manly either, but they're a necessity for the properly equipped tool box. A good set of utensils should include: a large firm plastic ladling spoon (you don't want a spoon that becomes wimpy as you're stirring steaming sauces or soups – THAT'S not manly, for sure), a straining spoon the same size, and a spatula. You can have wooden spoons if you wish, but don't get metal ones, especially if you have non-stick cookware. It's nice if you have a big wooden fork and spoon for salads – women seem to like that (makes big points). If you're making dinner for a woman for the first time, and you've remembered everything – warm rolls or garlic bread, you've set the table nicely, flowers are on the table in a vase you stole from some Italian restaurant, napkins are in the right place, the minestrone soups smells great and you put the salad on the table with a couple of cereal spoons, you've lost points even before dinner has begun. You might recover by having a dessert coffee and Bailey's, but I can assure you if you ever become a couple, she'll bring it up on your wedding night. Seriously.

Can Opener   ... A lot of guys equate hand-operated can openers with those metal things we had as kids that our depression-era parents bought that wouldn't take the dust off a can, let alone open it, the ones you had to squeeze so tight to make it work it left imprints or caused childhood arthritis. So, they go to the extreme and buy an electric can opener, thinking they've reached the pinnacle of perfection. Unfortunately, an electric can opener, and I don't care how much you spend on it or how well it works when you pull it out of the box, is doomed for failure. And watching someone trying desperately to get their electric can opener to work is like watching an SUV get stuck – you have to fight back a smile. SO, my recommendation on this piece of kitchen gear is to buy (or receive as a gift – bear in mind, it's much better to get this crap as a gift) a decent MANUAL can opener, one that has plastic coated handles. DON'T BUY THE ONES WE GREW UP WITH THAT ARE A LITTLE LESS EXPENSIVE AND HAVE METAL HANDLES.

Cookie Tray   ... Nothing can double as a cookie tray, so don't bother looking. And the uses for cookie trays go beyond the fairly obvious: they can also be used under anything you think might spill into your oven. Spilling in your oven means an eventual cleaning, so try your best to avoid this. Also, buy a good cookie tray, one with a non-stick surface. Why? Goes back to the less time in cleaning up drill.

Cutting Board   ... It's tricky to be cutting stuff on plates or on counter tops. I mean, the plates may be clean, but frozen chicken breasts or pork chops can get a little skittish on them. And using countertops, aside from their state of hygiene, aren't a good choice either (knife marks are frowned upon by landlords and real estate agents). No, the best way is to cut is on a cutting board. Wood is best from a bacteria-elimination perspective, although they require a touch more upkeep. These are easy to ask for as a gift, too.

Measuring Cup   ... These are essential, even with my casual approach to measuring ingredients. Get the glass ones because the plastic ones feel and look cheap, if for no other reason.

Any make of Auto Shut-Off Coffee Maker

... You know when you're driving downtown like a madman, late for your first appointment because one of your kids forgot their trumpet which they need for today's music class? And, as you're whipping through traffic you have this gnawing uncertainty: did I turn off the coffee maker? It's important to surround ourselves with products that think a little for themselves, as in, knowing when to shut themselves off.

Oven Mitts   ... Having burnt myself too many times using hand towels to retrieve cookies or something from the oven, I'm now a card-carrying spokesperson for the Oven Mitt Society. Get them.

Nice to Have ...

Containers for leftovers... Once you've taken the time to make the stuff, you might as well have the stuff to store it in. Ziploc Containers can be found in the bulk food section (don't ask me why) or in the sandwich bag section. If not, they're around somewhere, so ask. These are great if you don't eat enough margarine to have a good supply of containers for shepherd's pie, spaghetti sauce, soup, etc. They're really worth having because if you have to search high and low for a container to keep leftovers of the sauce you just made, you might be tempted to hurl it. And if you hurl it often, you're depriving yourself of two things: one, the wonder of leftovers, and two, the time needed to make something else for lunch tomorrow (to say nothing of the money saved).

Mini chopper   ... This is a perfect gift idea from your aunt who never knows what to send. A Mini Chopper is not that strategically essential to your kitchen set-up, but makes a terrific contribution the times you employ it. Toolbox equivalent? A socket set. You can get by without a socket set, but using it sure makes certain jobs much, much easier and . . . faster.

Indoor Grill   ... This device should be on the must-have side of the ledger, not because of the taste it generates but because of the size of the pancakes it can cook. It's also too damn handy being able to stay inside while barbecuing in the winter. The great thing about an indoor grill is it follows the rule of all *Cook Like A Mother!* devices: it can facilitate a decent tasting meal in a very short amount of time with the least amount of messing around. E.g., you come home from work on one of the nights you don't have the kids. The first thing you do is retrieve a frozen chicken breast from the freezer, get a potato, pull a stalk of broccoli from the fridge, and turn on the grill. While it's warming up you thaw the chicken in the microwave – don't over thaw it (do it a couple of times and you know why I'm warning against it) – chuck the chicken on the grill, microwave the potato, when the chicken's ready and the potato needs to cool down, there's the 3 minutes needed to cook your broccoli in the microwave. Presto, a tasty meal that's nutritious and ready in less than 20 minutes and the important thing, the texture and taste prove it didn't come out of a box. And you didn't freeze your ____ off outside in the winter.

Casserole Dish   ... Seriously. Having a decent casserole dish means you can make tuna casserole or some sort of hamburger rice dish that doesn't have a name. Besides, the kids like stuff that comes out of a casserole dish, generally speaking, of course.

RECIPES

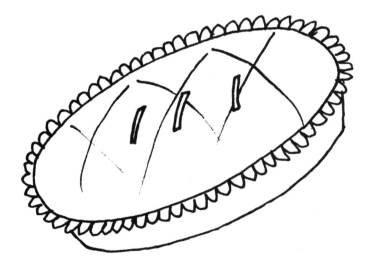

FAST
STUFF
TO
MAKE

Fast Stuff to Make

OK, so it's 5:45 Tuesday afternoon, you just walked in the door and you've got an hour and 15 minutes before the helicopter (*you wish*) arrives to take the kids to their activities that, of course, happen to be in as many different places as you have kids. Let's think for a minute, make something quick and tasty – you can read the mail when you get home after their activities. These meals can all be prepared and cooked quickly and still let you sit down, eat your meal and find out why that mean girl with the freckles tripped your little Sarah at recess.

Here's a meal that easy to complete, as long as a), you've got a food store nearby that sells barbecued chickens, and b), you don't mind stopping on the way home from work. The beauty to this meal is you save an hour, which is incalculable in terms of what else you can accomplish.

What you'll need: (besides the fricken' chicken):

Vegetables of choice

3 Potatoes

What you'll do:

1. Wash the potatoes, put them in the microwave for about 5 minutes for one, or 7 minutes for about 3. Don't forget to pierce the potatoes so you don't have splattered taters all over your microwave.
2. Once the potatoes are done, cook the vegetables. As the vegetables are cooking, cut up the chicken so everything is sort of ready at the same time.

For a real treat, you could bake some of those Pillsbury Crescent rolls, or make some toast.

Tips

1. I must admit that fresh vegetables are best; blind taste tests will confirm this. For a real time crunch, though, you can't beat yanking the frozen vegetables out of the freezer, putting them in a microwave-able dish, adding a little water.

2. While we're on the topic, always under-cook all vegetables at first – you can always cook for a minute more if you're breaking your teeth on the carrots – but I can't think of a better way of turning kids off vegetables quicker than by serving mushy, watery vegetables.

Note   This recipe is one of the reasons I got one of those Showtime Rotisseries. They only take 45 minutes to cook a 3 pound chicken.

Quick'n Chick'n

This is the weekday version of a Sunday roast chicken. It's becomes a Fast meal because it's done in the pressure cooker and takes just less than an hour to cook from start to finish, 5 minutes to prepare. It's a one-pot dish and it's got to be the fastest, tastiest, healthiest meal you can make. I'll admit making this meal takes a pretty high energy level, but it's worth it. I'll also admit that the first couple of times using the pressure cooker are a little stressful, mainly because there are a number of steps necessary and, if you're like me, you don't want to screw up. That said, the T-Fal pressure cooker is as close to foolproof as you can get. The pressure cooker comes with a recipe book that you can use or you can follow this one.

What you'll need:
> 3 lb. chicken,
> 3 fairly large potatoes
> 2 carrots
> salt and pepper
> powdered vegetable stock (Knorr has a line of stocks in little tins
>   that are great)
> 2 cups of water

What you'll do:
1. Follow the instructions on the label and clean the bird (see Tip 1 on next page).
2. Remove the giblet (it may have been removed; make sure by looking in the cavity and yelling "HELLO!" If there's an echo, the giblet's been removed. Just joking, by the way).
3. Make sure chicken is one of those "secured" ones that have a string holding the wings and drumsticks firmly. Otherwise, you have to tie it up.
4. Add two tablespoons of olive oil to the cooker. Turn heat to medium.
5. Brown all sides of the chicken once the oil is hot (see tip on page 30).
6. Once browned, remove it, drain off oil and insert trivet into bottom of cooker.
7. Place chicken squarely on top of trivet. It shouldn't be falling off or touching the sides.
8. Add 2 1/2 cups of water (see Tip 5).

Peter Wright

9. Sprinkle salt and pepper on chicken.
10. Attach and secure cover.
11. Turn the element to high.
12. When pressure cooker starts steaming (it's supposed to, don't worry), set timer for 24 minutes (8 minutes per pound). It takes a few minutes to start steaming.
13. Turn the oven on, set to 350 F.
14. Turn element down to about 6 1/2 to 7 1/2 (as in, medium high).
15. When the timer goes, turn off the element and remove. Follow instruction booklet on releasing steam.
16. When pressure cooker lid is available to open, transfer chicken to something that can go in the oven, like a cookie tray or something. Then put into the oven.
17. Set timer for 15 minutes.
18. While chicken is browning, place the steamer that comes with the pressure cooker on top of the trivet. Make sure there is still enough liquid to cover the trivet.
19. Add potatoes which you've quartered, and the carrots, which you've cut into 1-inch pieces.
20. Put the lid back on, put the element to high and bring the sucker back up to steam.
21. Cook for 7 minutes.

The chicken and the vegetables will be ready at the same time. You've been very busy during the hour, but now you've got 15 minutes to eat a good dinner.

Tips

1. To wash the chicken (or turkey, for that matter), you should use cold or warm water, not hot – just wash it the way you would a muddy football. Don't scrub too vigorously or you'll tear the skin.

2. Avoid food-borne diseases by washing your hands immediately after you've touched raw chicken with your hands (presumably the last time before it begins cooking, otherwise you'll spend a lot of time continually washing your hands).

3. Don't use anything, like a knife, cutting board, serving spoon, etc., that has had raw chicken on it for anything else until you've cleaned it thoroughly – and a cursory wipe with a dish cloth won't do it. See *Stuff Worth Knowing* for more hygiene info.

4. To avoid touching the raw chicken unnecessarily, when the recipe asks for browning of the entire bird, use a couple of rigid utensils, e.g., salad servers (wash them really well before using them). Otherwise, you have to use your hands. Gross.

5. Add flavor by using a cup of vegetable broth as part of the water.

6. The first few times you use a pressure cooker, observe the steam. Make sure it's a steady steam, not sputtering and not a fricken geyser; adjust heat accordingly.

7. Browning a chicken is more like searing the thing on all sides, so be prepared to keep moving it around the pot – just leave it in one place only for a few moments.

Cooking with a wok is almost a fail-safe method of cooking healthily and tastily (is there really such a word?). The reason I think woks are great, especially for us guys, is because it doesn't really matter what things look like going in, things don't have to be cut uniformly and all that presentation stuff. The smaller the pieces, the quicker you can eat, though, so keep that in mind. Of course, if you're cooking a meal for a first date, you can make a big show about how adept you are with a sharp knife, something that impresses less skittish women. This is one of my boys' and my favorite meals because it's extremely tasty, extremely quick and extremely nutritious.

What you'll need:
    1/2 lb beef sirloin cut into strips
    2 stalks of broccoli
    1 large stalk of celery
    1 large carrot
    1 medium onion
    1 of each green and red pepper
    1 – 2 tablespoons of Soya sauce
    2 cups of instant rice

Note: Your supermarket probably sells packages of beef steak that's been cut into strips for easy stir-frying. Get half a pound, or, if we shop at the same store, buy the smallest package – usually a pound, and freeze half. The beauty of the wok is you're able to use a fraction of what you think you'd need. The only spice you need, of course, is Soya sauce.

What you'll do:
1. Cut the beef strips into bite size pieces.
2. Cut the vegetables into bite size pieces: Slivers for everything but the onions, which you'll cut into rings.
3. Put the element on high and add 2 tbsp of cooking oil into the wok and heat up.
4. As the oil is heating up, measure the rice (equal parts rice and water – the box will tell you how much for the number of people you're feeding).
5. Once the oil is hot, add the beef and the rest of the onions.

6. As the beef is almost thoroughly browned, start the rice in a covered dish in the microwave.
7. Once the meat is browned (take a piece out and test it by cutting it in half) then, dump in the rest of the vegetables and STIR FRY, baby!
8. After 1 minute or so of stir frying, add the Soya sauce.
9. Cook for 4 minutes for firm vegetables, 6 for mushier ones.

As soon as the rice is ready, turn off the wok's element. Serve the rice with the beef and vegetables. Leave the Soya sauce on the table in case you need to add to the rice or wok dish.

Tips

1. Stir frying, surprisingly, means you keep "stirring" while the food is frying. You shouldn't leave stuff in one place for too long.

2. Don't put in so much Soya sauce or water that you're boiling everything, in effect.

3. As long as the meat is properly cooked, it doesn't really matter how long you cook the vegetables, obviously, the less time, the crunchier, the more time, the mushier.

4. Don't use olive oil with wok cooking; doesn't work well, don't really know why.

5. Chuck an onion ring in the bottom of the wok as it heats up, to give you an idea of when the thing has heated up enough to add the beef.

6. Don't be tempted into making a salad with this meal; doesn't go well.

7. What does go well is some toast from French or Italian bread.

Another Note: You can make 3 other meals using the wok basics: substitute chicken or pork for beef, use potatoes instead of rice, or no meat, just vegetables with rice or potatoes.

If you're like my kids and me, this is a meal you'll make a thousand times. For some reason (I guess for the mundane reason that it's tasty and comforting), my kids never tire of it – nor do I, for that matter. It will be a sorry day indeed when my sons tell me to cook anything other than pasta. This meal is our staple meal, the meal we default to. As a matter of fact, this meal is the reason why I buy my lean ground beef in bigger formats, so I can separate it into sections, put them into sandwich bags and freeze them. So each time I'm in a time-jam, but still want to make something I know will be good and the kids will like, I drag one of the frozen ground beef packets out of the freezer.

Each one of the big slabs makes about 10 packets of ground beef. This will give you an idea of how little ground beef I use in this recipe and every recipe that involves ground beef – it must be less than a 1/2 pound instead of the pound recipes usually call for. In case you're wondering, I've always been oriented towards vegetables more than meat, reasoning that it would be easier to keep weight down by using meat sparingly – so you can just as easily make this recipe without meat. But most of the meals we grew up with, of course, featured meat. It's also important for kids to have the protein they need (I know, there are other foods that can provide kids and us with protein, but, frankly, I can't be bothered), so while I make meals that include meat, I generally use less than most people.

What you'll need:
> 1/2 pound of lean ground beef
>> (you could use a pound if you wish)
>
> 1 jar of pasta sauce
> 1 medium onion
> 1 stalk of celery
> 1 green pepper
> 1 red pepper
> 1 clove of garlic
> 1 – 3 shakes of oregano, basil and pepper

What you'll do:

1. Wash the vegetables.
2. Cut them into workable sizes.
3. Chop garlic (if you have the time and the tools).
4. Heat up olive oil in skillet on 3/4 heat.
5. Give the vegetables a little (1 minute) head start in the skillet before adding the meat.
6. Add meat. Brown everything thoroughly. (Most recipes recommend draining off the oil, for obvious reasons. Sometimes I do, sometimes I don't. It tastes better when you don't. Of course, I'm using extra lean ground beef).
7. Add pasta sauce.
8. Cover. Turn down heat to 1/4 heat and simmer for 20 minutes.

Tips

1. The size and shape of the vegetables you cut should be influenced by the ages of your children: the younger they are, the smaller the pieces.

2. Everyone seems to know that spaghetti sauce tastes better the second day, so try to make far more than you think you'll use and either freeze or refrigerate (see chapter Stuff Worth Knowing for how long leftovers can be safely kept in the fridge).

3. Prepared pasta sauces certainly cost more than "tomato sauce," but they're quicker because you don't have to add lots of spices and do the "spice-to-taste" thing. For the real homemade taste, though, adding your own spices is the route to go.

4. If you want an unbelievable treat, use leftovers from a pot roast instead of ground beef.

(or Hamburger Helper if you're really rushed and no women are expected)

This is among the most comforting meals known to man and children. I'll admit it's extremely similar to pasta in a simple sauce, but this version cooks the pasta in the sauce, which makes it very, very tasty. It's important to note that if you're in a real mental slump and don't feel like expending the incredible amount of brain power this recipe demands, consider Hamburger Helper (I'm serious). Using HH means you don't have to add your own spices, which can cause low-level anxiety. Either way, whether you go the Heaven or Helper route, you can make each very tasty with the following directions. This is a great meal to make toast with or have really fresh bread with. I've found with these kinds of prepared dinners, you can use them as a foundation for some minor enhancements that make them at least a little healthier than they'd be without any vegetables.

What you'll need:

    1/2 pound of lean ground beef
    1 jar of prepared pasta sauce, not tomato sauce (needs more spices)
    1 can of crushed tomatoes (doesn't matter what size – big if you like tomatoes)
    1/2 of one green and red pepper each
    1 medium onion
    2 stalks of celery
    1 chopped clove of garlic, if you're ambitious and have the time
    1 cup of water
    2 tbsp (that's tablespoons to us) olive oil
    1 1/2 cups of pasta – your choice, preferably a thin noodle

What you'll do:

1. Wash all vegetables.
2. Cut the vegetables into workable sizes.
3. In a fairly deep skillet, add 2 tbsps of olive oil. Turn on element to 3/4 full.
4. When oil is up to temperature, add the garlic and onions. Brown quickly. Be careful not to let them burn by leaving them in one place too long. Two minutes should be fine.

5. Add meat, peppers and celery. Brown everything. Stir frequently. Browning should take 3 – 4 minutes. Drain or blot grease.
6. Once browned, add the pasta sauce, crushed tomatoes and the water. Then add the pasta, ensuring the pasta is completely covered by the sauce.
7. Cover and cook for 15 – 20 minutes.
8. Stir occasionally.

Or, for the Hamburger Helper version follow the instructions on the box after the meat browning part – and add whatever water they indicate plus 1/4 cup more because you're putting their pasta and some of your own in (about 1/4 cup more). Each version takes about 20 minutes to cook once the noodles are in.

Tips

1   Give your eyes a break: instead of the usual way of cutting vegetables, cut them on a diagonal – like they do in fancy restaurants. This way, you could make the same meal two days in a row and the kids will think it's a different meal.

2   If you got the Handi Chopper for a gift, drag it out, peel some garlic and give it a whirl. All meals are SO much better with fresh garlic.

3   The sizzling sound of a small piece of vegetable in the oil as it heats up will tell you when it's up to temperature.

Sloppy Joes

Apparently everyone but me knew how to make this. It's easy. All you have to do is when you follow the recipe for pasta sauce, make more than you need, because all Sloppy Joes are is spaghetti sauce on top of toast. They also have Sloppy Joe mixes available in your grocery store. I haven't tried them; they probably make the mix a lot more spicy and less tomatoey than my kids or I like. Add some celery or carrots on the side to increase the nutritional component. Don't forget to toast the bread unless your kids like really Sloppy Joes.

Tip

1   If your kids get tired of Sloppy Joes that taste like spaghetti sauce, add half a packet of the mix to your spaghetti sauce leftovers – gives it a different taste.

Hamburger Soup

Kids love this. It's easy and fast to make. It's also one of those things that you can be quite casual with measurements, make as much as you can and either chuck it into the freezer or fridge. My soup never makes it to the freezer because my boys and I have about 2 bowls each, which leaves very little to refrigerate, let alone freeze.

What you'll need:

> 1 1/2 lbs of lean ground beef
> 1 medium to large onion
> 1 large can peeled tomatoes
> 3 celery stalks
> 1 can of tomato soup
> 12 tablespoons of barley
> 2 cans of consommé
> 4 carrots
> 1/2 teaspoon thyme
> 2 cups of water

What you'll do:

1. Finely chop up the onion, carrots and celery.
2. Brown meat and onions. Drain well.
3. Hurl everything – the stuff you've cooked as well as the uncooked ingredients – into a large pot.
4. Simmer COVERED for at least 2 hours.

Tip

1 Make sure it's not boiling like a madman when you leave it, otherwise you'll have a different meal: burned hamburger goulash.

This is a recipe my girlfriend's parents got from their grandparents on Cache Lake, Ontario, close to the Manitoba border. It comes from an old Indian recipe (or so I'm told) that was only served to braves who were going out on their first date with the tribe's best looking gal. It's rumored to have magical powers, but I can't say what they are or the powers get reversed, something one really doesn't want to have happen.

What you'll need:

> 1 1/2 lbs of lean ground beef
> 1 small can of cream corn
> 1 small can peeled tomatoes
> 1 cup of Uncle Ben's rice
> 1 cup of water

What you'll do:

1. Cook rice first (7 minutes in the microwave, double that on the stovetop). Set aside.
2. Cook ground beef, drain, add rice, corn, tomatoes, mix well.
3. Cook on medium heat 15 minutes, stirring occasionally. Salt and pepper to taste.

Tip

1   The longer these types of meals simmer, the better they taste.

Shepherd's Pie

This is one of those tasty meals that everyone loves. The way I prepare this meal could be considered cheating because I buy the frozen Shepherd's Pie from my grocery store, but we're covered by the 6th Amendment: What I do to make a tasty meal in the least amount of time cannot be held against me. I'll give the recipe for Shepherd's Pie in the next chapter, in case you want to cook one from scratch, but the beauty of the frozen ones is threefold: 1, they seem to be quite tasty; 2, the kids love them; 3, there's usually leftovers; and the silent 4th real reason: they're FAST! And, the time you save on preparing a Shepherd's Pie from scratch can be put into the little things, the personal touch that we have observed is a trait of Cooking like a Mother. Meaning, you can make some Crescent Rolls and add a vegetable to be served on the side.

What you'll need:

> Frozen shepherd's pie – family size. Don't buy the individual sized ones, they're not as good as the full size ones for some reason.
> 1 or 2 stalks of broccoli
> Pillsbury Crescent rolls

What you'll do:

1. Follow the instructions on the box.
2. Use the timer. Set the timer to go off about 15 minutes early so you can get the broccoli ready (wash and cut into cookable sizes).
3. Once the broccoli is ready, whack open the crescent rolls (or get one of your kids to do it), put them on a cookie sheet and time it for when there's 12 minutes left for the shepherd's pie.
4. Start the broccoli only after the timer for the Shepherd's Pie has gone off because it only takes 3 minutes in the microwave.

Everything is ready at the same time, serve and enjoy.

Pizza Night

One night a week, say, Friday, make it pizza night. Kids love predictability, and pizza night is the easiest way to provide it. Call the same place, order the same thing. Do NOT introduce something new to this night, as in ordering from somewhere else, ordering something else, or inviting other people UNTIL the kids beg you to do so.

What you'll need:

1 decision on type of pizza
1 phone, plugged in
1 $20 bill, accessible
1 agreed-upon movie
1 bottle of wine/6 pack of beer (for you!)

What you'll do:

1. Get the movie first.
2. Call for the pizza.
3. Open the wine/crack open a pint.
4. Start the movie.
5. Put the movie on pause when the pizza arrives.
6. Resume the movie once you've paid.
7. Eat the pizza during the movie.

TASTY
STUFF
TO
MAKE

Tasty Stuff to Make

Fortunately after every work week comes a weekend, a time when we're allowed to move a little slower. These meals reflect our weekly slowdown. Not that these meals take forever to prepare and cook, some of them only take about 15 minutes to prepare, but they can't be done in the same blistering fashion as our Fast Stuff.

Minestrone Soup

I'm the first to admit this soup is extremely high on the Upfront Work Required scale. Minestrone soup and beef stew are the highest on the UWR scale, but also the tastiest. So, my only recommendation on this is you evaluate the circumstances under which you will make this soup very carefully. This is the sort of soup you could make for a first date, because a high UWR rating shows well, as it were. This is the sort of soup you could make if this date becomes a steady relationship and you wish to surprise her for her birthday, or some special weekend when it's just the two of you. And, of course, this is the sort of soup you could make if you're in trouble with said girlfriend as a peace offering. This is not, however, the sort of soup you make for your 2 boys under the age of 10, because they will not distinguish the 45 minutes it took to prepare the ingredients of this soup, let alone the actual cooking of it, from the 4.5 minutes it would take to heat up a can of vegetable soup. Try it, if you don't believe me. And I don't mean to sound motherly here, but remember when you were a kid and you were really interested in getting back to your friends outside and you hurt your mother's feelings day in, day out, because of your callous disregard for her efforts? It turns out that feeling is not gender-specific, it's universal: we can feel it too. And it's a crappy feeling. So, like I said, choose the applications for this soup carefully.

What you'll need:

    1 small turnip

    4 leeks

    2 celery stalks

    1 medium onion

    3 green beans

    2 tomatoes

    1 tablespoon of tomato paste (get the stuff that comes in a reusable tube)

    4 cups of hot vegetable stock

    2 oz of any small pasta (shell, elbow, doesn't matter – you could even use spaghetti as long as you break it into 1-inch strands)

Cook Like A Mother! Clean Like A Pro! 45

What you'll do:

1. Dice the turnip.
2. Thinly slice the leeks.
3. Chop the celery.
4. Peel and dice the carrots.
5. Slice the green beans into 1-inch pieces.
6. Peel and chop the tomato.*
7. Add 2 tablespoons of olive oil to the pressure cooker.
8. Add turnip, leeks, celery and carrots and panfry for about 5 minutes.
9. Once that's done, add the beans, tomatoes, a tablespoon of the tomato paste. Add the 4 cups of vegetable stock.
10. Cover, seal and bring to full steam.
11. Cook for 25 minutes. If you're using the T-Fal Clipso pressure cooker, release steam slowly, by removing from heat, allowing the steam to run out completely at the 2 position, turning the dial to 1, allowing the steam to release fully at that level, then to the Release steam position.
12. Uncover, add pasta and bring to a boil, stirring occasionally. Continue boiling, uncovered for 15 minutes.

Tips

1 Set the oven for 200. Put a loaf of crusty bread in the oven when the pasta is added to the soup.

2 If you have grated cheese lying around in the fridge, use it on the soup.

3 Panfry just means you let it fry for a moment in, oddly enough, a pan, and turn – and so on and so on … (don't ask me the difference between panfry and stir fry).

* Major Tip   To peel a tomato, apparently, you have to boil it for about 4 minutes until the skin looks like it's ready to come off, take it out of the water with a spoon to avoid burning yourself and, using a fork, gently peel off the skin.

Peter Wright

This toast is a bit high on the UWR scale, but it's really good and the kids love it. And it kind of has to be done this way, don't try to do it in reverse order because the end result is different. Don't believe me? Try it.

What you'll need:
> 6 slices whole wheat bread
> Shakeable parmesan cheese
> Oregano
> Garlic salt
> Butter or margarine (try to find the un-hydrogenized oil
>   margarine)

What you'll do:
1. First, use margarine or butter to spread on the whole wheat bread (trying to be healthy you know, you could use white bread).
2. Sprinkle on some shakeable parmesan cheese – enough to cover it lightly.
3. Sprinkle some oregano, then some garlic salt.
4. Then toast. This, of course, is presuming you have a toaster oven.

I've never tried this Tasty Toast in a vertical toaster, and I think it's easy to see why. It might best be left until someone gives you a toaster oven for Christmas rather than having to clean out the bottom of your vertical toaster.

Anyway, if you want to give the kids a treat and impress the mother of one of the kids you coach in soccer, this toast is a great, easy way of doing so.

Tip

1   Oddly enough, these steps have to be in this order. The cheese has to harden a little and the oregano has to get a little crispy.

Texas Style BBQ Baked Beans

Here's a perfect meal to make after a day outside as a stand-alone meal with crusty bread and a salad, or as a side dish to roast beef and vegetables.

What you'll need:

> 2 large (19 oz) cans baked beans
> 1/2 cup smoked flavor BBQ sauce
> 1/2 cup brown sugar (now the kids are interested!)
> 1 generous shake of Worcestershire sauce

What you'll do:

1. Put the beans in a medium or large saucepan.
2. Heat until bubbling.
3. Add all other ingredients. Stir well.
4. Cook for 10 minutes.

Peter Wright

Barbecued Salmon Steak

Looking over my recipes I realize fish is very under-represented. The reason for this is as simple as it is stupid. As you may have noticed by now, I'm not that organized. I tend to make meals that I can somehow have the ingredients in the house and use as needed. For me, fish does not fall into that category. It could be argued that the best way to cook fish is from fresh, at least that's the way I would prefer to cook it; every time I try to thaw fish it seems to go gross on me. On the other hand, there's nothing as tasty – and healthy, it turns out – as a barbecued salmon steak. Salmon and tuna are very high in omega 3 fatty acids, something that sounds nasty but turns out to be very good as a cancer-fighting component. If you don't have a BBQ, then grill it on the indoor grill. If you don't have an indoor grill, poach it. If you don't have an oven or toaster oven, fry it. If you don't have a fry pan, do it in your T-Fal Gourmet Skillet. If you don't have a Gourmet Skillet . . . ok, so what do you have?

What you'll need:
> Salmon steaks (one per person)
> 2 stalks of broccoli
> potato (1 per person)

What you'll do:
1. Wash the broccoli and cut them into 2 inch pieces. Put them into a microwave-safe dish, add a couple tablespoons of water.
2. Wash the potatoes.
3. Lightly brush the salmon steaks with olive oil to prevent them from drying out too much on the barbecue.
4. With the BBQ on medium heat, put the salmon steaks on. Hang with them while they cook on one side for about 5 minutes.
5. When you turn them over, dash inside and put the potatoes in the microwave for 7 minutes.
6. Dash back outside, continue cooking for another 5 minutes.
7. Take the steaks off the grill.
8. Once the potatoes are done, put the broccoli in for 3 minutes.
9. Open the potatoes, put some butter on each one and put onto the table.
10. Serve the broccoli as soon as it's done.

A Serious (read Health-related) Note
... about cooking fish

Grilling

Grilling is the testiest (and maybe tastiest) of traditional fish-cooking methods, because it is deceptive in its apparent simplicity. It's testy because you have to make sure they're properly cooked by constantly testing them. Our level of cooking tends to assume that grilling fish requires only as much attention as grilled steak, burgers or chicken; this is a serious misjudgment. Unlike other meats, fish tend to secrete much of their moisture when cooked, and on an open grill, the fish will just drip, drip, drip onto the coals. To preserve a fish's moisture, there are a couple steps that can be taken. First, coat the fish with oil. Oil will seal a portion of a fish's moisture inside. Second, keep careful watch over the fillets and flip them as soon as a cut into the fish reveals that the fish is cooked at least 1/2 way through. Once flipped, watch the fillets closely and remove the fish from heat as soon as it is cooked through. Another option is to place the fish on, or wrap the fish in, aluminum foil. The foil will capture the moisture and allow the fish to marinate in its moisture while cooking. I personally don't like this method – too moist for me – but it gives you a choice.

Tip

1   Do the vegetable and potato preparation before you put the salmon steaks on; they're so expensive you don't want to leave them unattended in case they get burnt or overdone.

Tuna Casserole

It's unbelievable how good this meal is and how simple it is to make. It's so simple, I can't believe how long it took me to figure it out. My mother gave me the recipe so many times, she got mad at me. I think it was more a matter that Tuna casserole is one of those meals Mothers have made millions of times and they can't explain the recipe. Mind you, my mother's at the age where people get annoyed when asked questions – let alone about cooking, so it's probably a good thing I wrote it down this time.

What you'll need:

Pasta	(bowtie, shell, elbow – something small);
Tuna	(buy the Flaked or Chunk White Tuna; don't get sucked into buying the Light tuna because you think it has less fat; it really has less goodness; it's kind of like the hotdog or sausage of tuna)
	1 can of Cream of Broccoli soup
	1/2 cup frozen peas
	grateable cheese, usually cheddar
Topping	some people put crumbled chips, crackers or even bread crumbs on top (but, then again, some people are odd, too)

What you'll do:

1. First cook the pasta.
2. Drain it, then put it into an oven dish that's big enough to hold however much pasta you have to cook for the number of people you're cooking for.
3. Once in the oven dish, mix in a can of tuna, throw in the frozen peas, pour in the can of soup, add the cheese on top and whatever you've chosen to finish off with – ground chips (mushed in your hand, it doesn't have to be some sort of complicated, intricate grinding process).
4. Put it into the preheated oven, set at 325° F for 25 to 30 minutes.

Then scoop it into pasta bowls. For soft textured meals like this one, consider making toast or having crunchy bread.

Pete's Pork Chops

Anyone can slap some chops on the grill, but what separates us as Mothers of Ingestion is how we can make them taste great without too much effort. These pork chops are unbelievable.

What you'll need:

> 2 tablespoons margarine or butter
> 1 teaspoon finely chopped fresh garlic
> 8 (1/2-inch thick) pork chops
> 1 (28 ounce) can whole peeled tomatoes, undrained, chopped into
>> 1-inch pieces
> 1 teaspoon dried basil leaves
> 1 teaspoon salt
> 1/2 teaspoon pepper
> 1/2 cup water
> 3 tablespoons cornstarch
> 1 green pepper, sliced in rings
> 1 onion, thinly sliced into rings

What you'll do:

1. Melt margarine or butter in large saucepan until sizzling; add chopped garlic.
2. Chuck in the chops.
3. Cook over medium-high heat. Turn occasionally, until browned on both sides (4 to 6 minutes).
4. Repeat with remaining chops. Remove all chops from pan; set aside.
5. Once all chops are browned, add tomatoes, basil, salt and pepper.
6. Bring to a boil – about 3 – 4 minutes. Stir occasionally.
7. Chuck the chops back into pan. Reduce heat to low, cook covered until chops are thoroughly cooked (no pink inside), about 45 – 55 minutes.
8. Remove chops; keep warm.
9. Mix water and cornstarch in small bowl. Stir into hot tomato mixture.
10. Add green pepper and onion.
11. Increase heat to medium-high. Cook until mixture is thickened and vegetables are nicely crisped (about 5 to 6 minutes). Stir occasionally.

Serve over the chops. A really good addition to this is scalloped potatoes and green beans.

So, everyone's tired of pot roasts, roast beef, pasta, fish, shepherd's pie, tuna casserole, beef stew, anything barbecued, etc., etc., etc.? Well, then, it's Pork Roast Thyme. This is so tasty and different, you'll be back to the well-trodden cooking ground in no thyme.

What you'll need:

       5 pounds pork roast, fat trimmed
       3 cloves garlic, sliced
       1 teaspoon salt
       1 1/2 teaspoons ground black pepper
       3 bay leaves
       1/2 cup cider vinegar
       1 teaspoon dried thyme

What you'll do:

1. Preheat oven to 325° F.
2. With a small knife, pierce top of roast. Force garlic slices into the cuts.
3. Sprinkle the roast with salt and pepper.
4. Place bay leaves in the bottom of the roasting pan, and set roast on top of bay leaves, fat side up.
5. Mix vinegar and thyme in a small bowl, and pour over the top of the roast.
6. Bake in the preheated oven 3 hours, or until an internal temperature of 160° F is reached.
7. Using a baster or spoon, baste the drippings over the roast frequently while it is cooking.
8. Let the roast cool for 10 minutes when done before slicing.

Tip

1   The "fat side up" refers to the fact that most roasts come with a great slab of fat attached by string to one side. If your roast doesn't have it, then, of course, if doesn't matter. Next time if you go to buy a roast and it's missing, ask the butcher person to add a slab – really improves the taste.

Yer Traditional Roast Chicken

For the longest time, my stove was an only child. I knew it was related, closely, in fact, to the oven, but I just wasn't comfortable making friends with this almost out-of-reach, difficult-to-understand acquaintance. But, recently I decided the worst thing my oven could do would be to wreck my dinner and burn down my house, so I decided to use it more frequently. Once you get over a common apprehension to use an oven (maybe it's just me), you can make some terrific meals. One of them that serves really well as a testing ground for cooking a Christmas turkey is a small roast chicken.

You get exposed to basting, which is something I never really thought I'd do in my life. You also get exposed to brushing olive oil all over a raw chicken, something I also never thought I'd get a chance to do (and something that, frankly, is as gross as it sounds). Lastly, you get a chance to extract from a chicken's butt a white little bag that contains its innards, something I never, ever, ever thought I could do, let alone repeatedly. But, once you've done it, there's very little you can't do. First Aid's a snap after you've rooted around a poultry cavity trying to get a grip on a slippery little bag that you really don't want to rip. But anyway ...

What you'll need:
> 3 pound chicken
> 2 broccoli stalks
> 2 cups of instant rice
> salt, pepper, oregano

What you'll do:
1. Clean the chicken by running it under cold or warm water and gently scrubbing.
2. Preheat the oven to 325°F.
3. Sprinkle garlic salt, pepper, oregano and paprika if you have some. Not too much, just enough to make it look like you've added some spices.
4. If you have very little to do and have an extra minute, lightly brush the chicken with olive oil which makes the skin turn a nicer shade of brown and makes it taste better.
5. Cook the bird for 25 minutes a pound.

Peter Wright

6. Set the timer to go off about 10 minutes early so you can put the instant rice in.
7. Once your rice is cooked, remove it from the microwave and put the broccoli in.
8. Cook broccoli for 3 minutes.

About 15 minutes before the chicken is ready, get your kids to set the table and get yourself or your dinner companion to open the wine. Once the final buzzer goes, drag the chicken out of the oven (have I mentioned oven mitts yet?), and carve. Your rice is still hot, the broccoli is perfect, and you're sitting down to a tasty, nutritious meal that everyone will enjoy.

Tips

1   Use a fresh chicken. You think trying to extract the bag of giblets is tricky to remove from a fresh chicken, wait until you try to get a grip on a semi-frozen bag and pull it out without tearing it. Having to worry about whether the bird has been properly thawed isn't worth the small savings they offer.

2   The best way to do broccoli is to use mainly the "flowers', the top of the stalk, cut them into almost bitesize pieces (depending on the age of your children), put them in some sort of microwaveable bowl and add just enough water as though you were trying to cover the bottom with water. It amounts to a couple of tablespoons, but a splash of water will do it. Cover the broccoli with either wax paper, a side plate turned upside down, or an actual cover if you're really organized.

Pot Roast Pronto

This is a great thing for Sunday night dinners, just like ol' Mom, or, for that matter, your ol' wife used to make. This pressure cooker version is surprisingly easy and quick to make and leaves time for other activities throughout the day. (I know I've mentioned it, but pressure cooking takes a third of the time of conventional cooking; I'll give instructions on how to cook a roast in a roasting pan following this pressure cooker version, but I highly recommend you get one – see the chapter Stuff to Make It In for rationale for having a pressure cooker). Frankly, my appreciation of pressure cookers is largely because I can have almost any meal I wish to cook and not have to change personalities, i.e., become a planner.

Case in point, I had some friends over for dinner recently and I actually bought the roast at 4:00 p.m., came home, prepared it, put it in the pressure cooker by 4:30 and we sat down to eat around 6:30. Conventional cooking of a roast would have it in the oven around 1:00 p.m. to eat at the same time – which, of course, isn't the end of the world unless you were busy engineering a touchdown. And, don't forget, you can make a nice change every now and then by leaving out the potatoes and using rice instead. The reason I use potatoes more often than not is because of our *Cook Like A Mother!* motto: make it fast, make it tasty. Using potatoes allows us to keep to one cooking device, the pressure cooker (or, for that matter, the roasting pan).

What you need:
>3 pound roast, usually a rump or sirloin cut
>2 large carrots
>1 onion
>4 medium potatoes

What you'll do:
1. In 2 tablespoons of olive oil, brown the roast on all sides.
2. Season it lightly with salt, pepper, garlic salt, and some oregano (can never forget the oregano!)
3. Remove the roast, leaving the oil and drippings.
4. Sauté the onions and leave in the pot.
5. Add the pressure cooker's trivet and place the roast on it.

6. Add at least 2 1/2 cups of liquid, some salt and pepper. For the liquids, use a cup of water, a cup of some sort of beef broth (hot water and Bovril or Oxo cube or Knorr beef stock), and a 1/2 cup of red wine.
7. Lock the top into place, bring to a steam, put the pressure cooker on 2, and once it's up to steam, it will take 35 minutes per pound to cook.
8. Set the timer to go off 10 minutes before this, so you can open it quickly (see instructions on how to release steam either quickly or slowly), and
9. Add the vegetables. They'll cook for the remaining minutes with the roast and give them that delicious taste, aroma and texture.

Tip

1   If you opt not to have potatoes and wish to have rice instead, once the roast is done, cook some rice. You can use the 5 minutes or so it will take to cook the rice to serve the roast and vegetables, and by the time you're ready to put the plates on the table, the rice will be ready.

Pot Roast Not-So-Pronto

The roasting pan version of this dinner is, frankly, a little tastier, but takes longer and involves, to my way of thinking anyway, more screwing around than the pressure cooked version. Both make the house smell great, which sounds unnecessary until you experience how comforting it is to walk into a house that has a roast cooking.

What you'll need:

> 3 pound roast, (sirloin, rump, inside round)
> 4 large carrots
> 5 potatoes
> 1 onion
> Salt, pepper, oregano

What you'll do:

1. Peel the carrots.
2. Wash and peel the potatoes.
3. Peel and cut the onion into sections.
4. Place the roast in the pan. Sear it on all sides. You can do this on top of the stove in the roasting pan.
5. When the all sides are brown, season it lightly with salt, pepper, garlic salt, and some oregano (can never forget the oregano!).
6. Add about 1/2 cup of water, 1 cup of beef broth (consommé, if you have it) and a 1/2 cup of red wine into the roasting pan.
7. Put the covered roasting pan into a preheated oven at 350 F. Set the timer for an hour a pound.
8. Take the cover off at the halfway point of cooking, add the carrots, onions and potatoes by placing them around the edges of the roast. Add more liquid (a cup or so). Replace cover and put back in the oven. You shouldn't need a knife with this meal, except to butter some hot bread or Crescent Rolls.

You could put the vegetables in a bowl and put them, covered, into the oven while you're carving the roast, so they're still warm when you're ready to serve.

Periodically check the roast to ensure it's not running out of liquid. The important thing is with a pot roast you're after a certain texture – you want the beef to be able to fall off the roast.

Beef Stew

If you're a stew fan, you know that a hot stew on a cold fall or winter night is hard to beat. Of course, if you don't live in a cold climate I guess you wouldn't know how comforting a nice hot stew can be when you've just come in from tobogganing or shoveling the driveway, so maybe you're not a big stew fan. With a heated crusty loaf of bread and a bottle of wine, this is a top-rated meal on the comfort scale. If you are indeed a stew fan, you also know that the beef has to be so soft it melts in your mouth. It's like the stew version of pot roasted beef: no knife should be needed. This usually takes time, as in over 4 hours, which means starting dinner just after lunch, and very few guys I know can think about starting to cook supper early in the afternoon, and I am certainly no exception. Which means, of course, only one thing: this is a job for the pressure cooker. The only time-consuming component that can't be avoided, of course, is the preparation of the ingredients.

* UWR = Upfront Work Required. All cooking, of course, takes a certain amount of prep time, but these recipes are guaranteed to make you ask halfway through "Why am I doing this?" You have to keep telling yourself "it's going to taste great, it's going to taste great, it's going to . . . "

What you'll need:
> 1 3/4 lbs of beef chuck or round
> 3 leeks
> 2 carrots
> 1 large potato
> 1 onion
> 1 turnip
> 1 rib (stalk) of celery.

What you'll do:
1. Cut the beef into 3/4 to 1 inch pieces – even if you find a package of stewing beef.
2. Thinly slice the 3 leeks.
3. Peel the carrots, halve them lengthwise and cut into 1 inch pieces.
4. Peel the onion and slice into sections.
5. Peel the turnip and chop it coarsely, which means, in case you're wondering, as I did, that you make no special effort to cut them uniformly.

6. Slice the celery rib into 1/2 inch pieces.
7. Add 2 or 3 tablespoons of olive oil (a splash) to pressure cooker.
8. Add beef and brown over moderate heat.
9. Remove the meat leaving the residual oil and pan drippings.
10. Add the vegetables to cooker. Sauté vegetables until lightly browned, (almost 5 minutes of fairly constant stirring).
11. Add the browned beef, 2 cups of beef stock or broth, 1/4 cup of red wine, salt and pepper to taste.
12. Cover, lock and bring to full steam. Cook for 40 minutes.
13. Remove from heat. Release steam quickly.

Tips

1. Most supermarkets sell packages of stewing beef, but even if they don't, you can ask the meat person to cut some up for you. Just tell him/her that the size of the pieces of the packaged stuff is too big for your kids and before he can say "do it yourself, ya lazy . . ." say "thanks Buddy" and walk away looking at your grocery list with concentration. If your kids are with you, they can stay standing there smiling.

2. If you're expecting company for this meal, get this Upfront Work done upfront, otherwise you won't have much time to chat.

   OR If it's company with a Big C, she can help prepare the ingredients.

3. For cleaning leeks, peel a couple of layers off until you get to a level that doesn't have dirt, then wash.

4. For cutting leeks, begin cutting at the point where the stalk turns to leaf – we only want the stalk.

5. Peeling turnips is a lot like peeling a candle – very slippery. The easiest way is to not try to "peel" it, rather, slice off the waxy cover. It leaves a little less of the turnip to use but saves a huge amount of time.

6. When the pressure cooker begins to steam, set the timer for 30 minutes instead of the 40. When it goes off, put the bread into the oven pre-heated to 200 and then reset the timer for the stew's last 10 minutes. This will allow the bread to be nicely heated by the time your stew is ready.

7. Rice is a great addition to this meal: start microwave cooking 2 cups of instant rice at the same time you put the bread in the oven.

Peter Wright

Homemade Shepherd's Pie

Although we can easily buy this product in the frozen food section (as we did in Fast Stuff to Make), there are times you have to test yourself. There are times you just have to. Why? Because it's there, dammit. It's there to climb, jump, swim, make. Shepherd's Pie was also one of those meals my mom made all the time that everyone loved. I never made one for myself until I wanted to test myself (sometimes it's fun to test yourself on something you know you'll win at). This is a real tasty meal and is easy to make.

What you'll need:

> 2 pounds of lean ground beef (or the pot roast leftovers)
> 1 cup of frozen corn and
> 6 large potatoes

What you'll do:

1. Wash and peel the potatoes.
2. Put them in a pot and boil for about 1/2 an hour.
3. Then, brown the ground beef (or the pot roast leftovers that you have kind of shredded into manageable pieces).
4. Drain off the excess oil and mix in the frozen corn. Stir well.
5. Transfer the mixture into an oven-ready casserole dish.
6. Once the potatoes are done, mash them with butter, and place on top of the meat/corn. Spread potatoes.
7. Sprinkle salt and pepper and maybe some . . .oregano!
8. Put into a preheat oven at 325° F for about an hour.

So, if we add these times up, we're about the same as a frozen shepherd's pie, which takes about 65–70 minutes. The only real difference is the time you'd have to spend preparing the handmade version, about 30 minutes or so if you're quick, versus, oh, 30 seconds it takes to rip open a package and put into the oven.

Tips

1   DON'T OVERCOOK BROCCOLI. It becomes too gross when it's mushy which is the single biggest reason kids don't like vegetables.

2   You can speed up the cooking time of boiling potatoes by cutting them into quarters.

A Delicious Casserole!

The exclamation mark is meant to assist you in how to say it when the kids ask, "What's for dinner?" And you can say, "A Delicious Casserole!" And they'll say, "What's in it?" And you'll say, "I'm too busy putting all of the ingredients in and I'm concentrating, so I'll tell you later." By which time, of course, you will have finished the casserole and you won't have had to tell them the meat was ground turkey. I'd never tell my kids we're eating ground turkey, everything's chicken or beef. We're using ground turkey for two reasons: it apparently is healthier for us because of lower fat, and it's generally less expensive. In all fairness, though, I'm not a big fan of ground turkey as it doesn't seem to cook the same way as ground beef, but try it for the health reasons. Then do the recipe using ground beef. If it gets a ho-hum reaction with the turkey and a solid "give me more" reaction with the beef, case closed. If using turkey gets the same response, then keep using the healthier ingredient. Also, I'm the first to admit there's far more ingredients in this recipe than most, but it's really good.

What you'll need:

> 1 lb of ground turkey (or lean ground beef)
> 16 oz box of multicolored (Rainbow) Rotini
> 1 can of diced tomatoes
> 2 tbsp olive oil
> 5 tbsp balsamic vinegar
> 2 cups of prepared pasta sauce
> 1 tsp dried basil
> 2 healthy shakes of garlic powder
> 1 small onion chopped
> 2 – 3 shakes Italian seasoning
> Shredded mozzarella cheese

What you'll do:

1. Brown the meat, garlic powder, chopped onions and basil.
2. Once well browned, add diced tomatoes with juice, olive oil, balsamic vinegar and Italian seasoning.
3. Simmer on low heat until most of the liquid is gone.
4. At the same time, cook rotini and drain.

Peter Wright

5. Combine the meat mixture, pasta, and the prepared pasta sauce and mix well.
6. Get the casserole dish out (the big one), spray it with Pam (if you have the olive oil Pam, use it), and put the entire mixture in the casserole dish.
7. Sprinkle a generous amount of the shredded mozzarella cheese over the whole mess and wing it into the oven (which has been preheated to 350F).
8. Cook for 35 minutes.

Tip

1   Rinse the pasta with cold water (otherwise it gets too sticky).

Dave's Prague Peppers
(Ground Beef or Turkey Stuffed Peppers)

Dave's a guy I went to high school with, who's over in Prague with his wife and kids. They're on some sort of top secret mission over there and his cover is a stay-at-home Dad. This is one of his kids' favorite recipes. I have to mention using ground beef or turkey because my sister tells me ground lamb is difficult to find and can be expensive, so govern yourself accordingly. Don't forget, when I say ground beef, I mean lean ground beef.

"This is a beauty and kinda fun 'cause you force the kids to eat at least one veggie!"

What you'll need:
>   4 red peppers
>   1 pound ground lamb, beef or turkey
>   salt and pepper
>   rosemary
>   rice
>   1 large (28 oz) can 'o tomatoes (whole)
>   1 onion
>   2 or 3 garlic cloves
>   olive oil
>   hot sauce

What you'll do:
1. Cook the meat until almost done (if it's overcooked it will be rubbery).
2. Put it aside.
3. Dice the onion and garlic and sauté in the olive oil.
4. Add the tomatoes, salt, pepper and rosemary to taste.
5. Simmer the whole mess until it is quite thick (yes, it is like making a tomato sauce).
6. While this is going on, cut the tops off the peppers and clean out the insides.
7. Prepare the rice.
8. Once the sauce is at the desired consistency, add the meat for about five minutes then throw in the rice.
9. Finally, stuff the peppers with the tomato, meat and rice business, place them in a pan that gives them enough support to stand up.

10. Heat the oven to about 350° F and cook the rascals for 30-45 minutes. A little Greek salad as a side works! (You're on your own here if you don't know how to make a Greek salad, because I don't either. Not being a big fan of feta cheese or olives, Greek salads don't rank high. A substitute salad would have balsamic vinegar dressing, though.

Tip

1   If you have too much sauce, prepare a few more peppers. They keep great in the fridge.

(Thanks Dave, see you at the reunion!)

My Two Sons' Pasta

Every once in a while we have to break out of the easy, established way of doing things. I must admit I default to cooking pasta with tomato sauce 9.9 times out of 10, if I'm stuck for something to make for dinner. I mean, if it works, don't fix it, and luckily the boys love my pasta sauce which is more than reasonably healthy. On the other hand, we should try to keep our eyes open to new things once in a while; this recipe is a perfect example of finding something good by accident.

After browning some garlic and onions in olive oil with green and red peppers, along with the chicken, I was all set to pour in my standard tomato sauce when I stopped, jar of Classico Sun-Dried Tomatoes poised in my hand while thinking about something. As I began to refocus on what I was doing, it dawned on me that it was time for a change – in life and the dinner I was making. I wanted the chicken, the vegetables and the olive oil – I wanted that taste and texture. But just this once I didn't want the ordinary. So, I added more olive oil and some vegetable stock (hot water in a cup with a spoonful of Knorr's Vegetable Stock). This meal is made with green and red peppers, onions and garlic, chicken, sautéed in olive oil and vegetable stock. It was great! And yes, the ultimate taste testers – my boys – gave it a hearty pass, which is measured, of course, by the fact that they had seconds.

What you'll need:
>1 or 2 boneless chicken breasts
>1 green pepper
>1 red pepper
>1 medium onion
>1 clove of garlic
>some olive oil
>vegetable stock (you can buy tins of Knorr Vegetable Stock in your grocery store – just ask for it)
>Pasta, preferably rotini

What you'll do:

1. Cut the chicken breasts into cubes.
2. Cut the peppers into thin strips.
3. Peel the garlic and chop into small pieces (dig out your Handi Chopper).
4. Cut the onions into sections.
5. Add 2 tbsp olive oil to your pan, heat. Sauté the onions.
6. Add the chicken and peppers and continue to sauté.
7. Put the water on to boil.
8. Once ingredients are browned, add a minor splash more olive oil and 1/2 cup of vegetable broth. Stir.
9. Put pasta in boiling water. Keep the sauce warm by covering and on low heat. Put toast on just as you're turning off the heat for the pasta, before you strain it.

Chocolate Pancakes

Why is this here? Because it's the weekend, your kids probably love chocolate, and frankly, not everybody would think of doing pancakes like this. This is certainly not a dinner recipe (even for Pancake Tuesday), just something that kids – especially between 5 and 8 who like chocolate – love. They're easy to make, too.

What you'll need:
> Aunt Jemima pancake mix (the Just-add-water one)
> 1 tablespoon of powdered Nestlé's chocolate milk mix

What you'll do:
1. Follow the directions on the box for the number of people you have.
2. Once the batter is ready (the lumps are gone), mix in the chocolate milk mix, as it were, until you have an evenly chocolate brown mixture.

Tip

1   A rule of thumb is to make more than you think you'll need for the simple reason it's a turbine pain in the ass to be really enjoying your pancakes and someone's one pancake short of the perfect breakfast and can't have more because you've run out of batter. And by the time everything is revved up again, somehow the moment, the enjoyment, the taste, the hunger, the kid – everything's gone. Of course, that's just my experience.

Blueberry Pancakes

Sometimes you gotta make stuff the gals like and since we're on the topic of pancakes, here's another pancake recipe but with a simple twist. Keep in mind, we're after simple and tasty. This is almost too simple, but it sure is tasty and VERY appropriate if someone has stayed the night (of course the kids aren't there!) and you'd like to maintain the illusion you're a together kind of guy, which might be compromised if she sits down to breakfast in your shirt (with a couple of buttons undone – but anyway, where was I?), and you give her a Barbie bowl and the box of Fruit Loops for breakfast.

What you'll need:
> Aunt Jemima pancake mix (the Just-add-water one)
> Frozen blueberries (or fresh if you just came back from berry picking. Not)

What you'll do:
1. Same drill: follow the directions on the box and make more than you think.
2. Throw the blueberries in once the batter is ready.

Peter Wright

THE
GOOD
STUFF

The Good Stuff

Recipes for Romance, AKA, The Good Stuff

There's a time and place for everything. You wouldn't serve a shepherd's pie on a first date. I don't know why, just wouldn't seem right. It's a little too slippers-off kind of meal. Conversely, you certainly wouldn't go to the trouble of preparing and serving Risotto to your kids after a soccer tournament. So, these recipes will be recognized for what they are: a tasty meal, a little sensual, a considerable amount of work, and, usually – if you've chosen correctly – well received.

All the ingredients for recipes in this section are for two people.

Caesar Salad

This is always a hit at dinner parties, just make sure everyone has some – it's pretty potent! It's also an aphrodisiac to some – yea, baby! (Caesar salad is certainly one of the most popular salads, especially if you're cooking for someone for the first time. Although I would tend to use a prepared Caesar salad dressing and toss in some croutons, this homemade recipe shows a much higher UWR* rating, something that may pay greater dividends).

What you'll need:

2 cloves garlic, finely chopped
3 anchovy filets, finely chopped (don't argue)
1 egg
2 teaspoons Dijon mustard
1/2 to 3/4 cup olive oil
1 – 2 tablespoons balsamic vinegar
Juice of half a lemon (can be substituted with 1 teaspoon
    concentrated lemon juice)
1 – 2 tablespoons grated Parmesan cheese
4 shakes of salt, 10 grinds of pepper
Dash of hot sauce
Romaine lettuce

What you'll do:

1. In a mixing bowl, add garlic, anchovies and the egg.
2. Whisk with a fork or, well, a whisk*.
3. While whisking, slowly pour in olive oil, then balsamic vinegar.
4. Don't substitute with another vinegar – if you don't have balsamic vinegar, don't add any.
5. Squeeze in the lemon juice and stir in the mustard, cheese and seasonings.
6. Adjust the seasonings to taste.
7. Just before serving, pour over shredded romaine and toss (the lettuce will wilt if it sits for long with the dressing on).

Tip

Err on the side of caution with the olive oil. You can add more if the dressing is too strong. If it is too weak, let the mixture sit in the fridge for up to a day to allow the flavors to infuse (which is good if you've planned ahead, otherwise Let the Games Begin!)

* Don't feel bad about not having a whisk. Studies show that fewer than .5 percent of male households have a whisk, this one included.

* Whisking is a way of saying stir quickly and lightly.

* UWR = Upfront Work Required. See recipe for Minestrone soup, Risotto for other UWR recipes.

Marinated Lemon Chicken

This is a meal that's easy to make and is more visually impressive than most meals. As we know, there are times you'd like to have something that not only tastes good, but looks good, too. Still, you don't have to be a gourmet cook to sometimes make something visually appealing. This is the sort of meal you'd serve if you're having another couple for dinner and you've had pasta for three nights in a row, made roast beef for them last time and had pot roast in your pressure cooker the time before that. The only caveat to this recipe is that you need to do Steps 1 to 7 no less than 2 hours before dinner (for the marinade to marinate).

What you'll need:

> 6 boneless chicken breasts (1 per person and maybe a couple
>> extra for lunch tomorrow or if someone really wants more)
> 1 lemon
> 1 of those plastic lemon-shaped juice things
> 2 cloves of garlic
> 1 each green, red and yellow peppers
> 3 cups instant rice
> generous sprinkle of oregano (surprise)

What you'll do:

1. Put the chicken in a container that is big enough to hold 6 breasts flat.
2. Pour about 1/2 an inch of olive oil into the bottom of the container over the chicken.
3. Finely chop or crush the garlic cloves and sprinkle all over the chicken.
4. Cut the lemon into half and using a fork, grind out the juice over the chicken allowing the occasional piece of lemon (doesn't matter if some seeds are included – it's just a marinade) to fall onto the chicken.
5. Pour a little (couple of squirts here and there – where you think you missed with the real lemon) of the lemon juice over the chicken.
6. Sprinkle the chicken with the oregano, trying to be even with your sprinkling.
7. Cover the container with plastic wrap and place in the fridge.
8. Wash the peppers and slice into big, thick strips, thicker than you'd do for sauces, so they won't fall through the grill on your BBQ.

9. Measure enough rice for the number of people you're having (follow the measurements on the box – it's usually equal parts rice, equal parts water). Measure the water but don't put it in.
10. Put the chicken on the barbecue to cook first, (don't be thinking I'm telling you to put whatever container you've got the chicken in on the BBQ!) Cook about 20 minutes.
11. When the chicken is nearly all cooked, grill the peppers for 2 minutes.
12. Remove chicken from BBQ and take inside.
13. While inside, start the rice in the microwave for approximately 7 minutes. Do this quickly because peppers can burn quickly. (Let the chicken finish cooking, take it off and take it inside. While you're inside, put the rice into the microwave for 7 minutes, return to the BBQ pretty quickly because you've put the peppers on high).

As you're walking in from outside, your rice should be ready, the chicken's cooked, the peppers are perfect and you can serve immediately.

Tips

1   If you sliced the peppers too thinly and they seem like they're going to fall through the grill, take the grate from your toaster oven out and put it sideways on the BBQ grill.

2   To leave grill marks on the peppers and not burn the chicken, move the chicken to one side, lower the heat (if you have a clean metal bowl, chuck them in there and leave on the BBQ). Put the peppers on the other side and turn the heat to high.

3   If you think you won't be able to get right back out to the BBQ because, say, you have to open the fridge, get a beer out, take off the cap and maybe pour it into a glass, have a chat with your guests and so on, don't put the BBQ on high until you're back out there and ready to put your attention to the peppers.

4   If you've planned it really well, the people or person you're having to dinner brought a salad, because a nice salad with balsamic vinegar really goes well with this meal – more so if you don't have to make it.

5   If you've unbelievably organized, you're supposed to turn the chicken over at least once while it's marinating in the fridge. I've never done this and can't imagine remembering, so there you go.

Peter Wright

This is the kind of meal you'd make someone you really think is top drawer. This meal shows you're more than capable of holding your own in the kitchen, and shows a nostalgic, homey side. Of course, to the wrong person, it shows you're a true blue carnivore without any sense of adventure, so if you get this reaction too often, save this meal for good company, small c, or change bowling alleys.

What you'll need:
> 4 pound roast (rump, sirloin tip or ask the butcher what they'd suggest for a roast)
> salt and pepper seasoning
> 2 stalks of fresh broccoli
> 4 carrots
> 4 potatoes

What you'll do:
1. Wash the broccoli and cut into 2-inch pieces.
2. Peel the carrots and cut into 2-inch pieces.
3. Wash and peel the potatoes.
4. Put the roast into the roasting pan. Season with salt, pepper, garlic powder.
5. Place it into the oven, preheated to 350F.
6. Cook for 30 minutes a pound. Use a meat thermometer to gauge the level of cooking.
7. Bake the potatoes (you'll have to calculate when to start them – they'll take about an hour).

Tip

1   Gravy. Some people like to do interesting things with the juices in the bottom of the roasting pan for gravy. I haven't paid terrific attention to this task, but here's what I remember: once you've removed the roast, put the empty roasting pan on an element on medium heat. It seems you want the juices to bubble while you add a little (a tablespoon or two) flour or corn starch and water to thicken. Keep stirring while adding these ingredients until everything looks smooth. If this sounds like too much work, buy one of those instant gravy mixes and follow the instructions on the package. I'd add whatever concoction those packages make to the juices in the pan for extra texture and flavor.

Tomato Steak

Most guys love steak, no question. Some women like steak, too. Sometimes, though, we need different ways of serving it. One of the easiest ways of using steak in a meal that doesn't involve the barbeque is using strips of steak in a wok. Another tasty use of steak is this recipe with a really appropriate twist: it combines steak with two other favorite food groups: spaghetti sauce and beer.

What you'll need:
- 1/2 cup rice, uncooked
- 1 tbsp olive oil
- 1/4 thinly sliced onions
- 1/2 lb extra lean sirloin strips
- 2 tbsp spaghetti sauce
- 1 tbsp steak sauce
- 1/2 cup spinach
- 1/4 cup beer

What you'll do:
1. Cook the rice according to the package directions.
2. Heat the oil in a non-stick skillet. Brown the onions and the sirloin over moderately high heat for about 10 minutes.
3. Add the sauces, spinach, and beer and simmer for 5 minutes. Serve over the rice.
4. For conservation purposes, drink the rest of the beer.

Tip

1   This seems like a no-brainer, but this is another one of those meals that you need either toast or Italian bread to accompany.

Pasta Putanesca

Here is an incredibly fast, incredibly cheap meal that tastes gourmet. My nephew tells me this pasta was reputedly a favorite of Italian "ladies of the night." It may be best not to share this with your date as you're serving it for dinner – unless your wallet's handy (I never asked him how he got this info!).

What you'll need:
> Your favorite pasta (rotini works well)
> 1 can diced tomatoes
> 2 cloves garlic
> 1 medium onion
> 1 can tuna
> Black olives – Kalamata are good (check the deli section, anything but canned will do)
> Capers (optional)
> Salt and pepper to taste

What you'll do:
1. Sauté the onion and garlic in olive oil over medium heat until translucent (clear).
2. Add diced tomatoes (for a thicker sauce, drain most of the juice from the can before adding tomatoes).
3. Add your favorite herbs (rosemary, basil, oregano, thyme, etc.) and freshly ground black pepper.
4. If you are having red wine with your meal, add a splash to the sauce.
5. Reduce heat and simmer until sauce begins to thicken.
6. Add tuna and olives (and capers if using).
7. Try not to stir too much or the tuna and olives will disintegrate.
8. Serve over top of your favorite cooked pasta.

You can replace the tuna with Italian sausage and have a dish that is just as tasty for those who don't like tuna.

Tip

1   Some people like to add a pinch of sugar to off-set the acidity of the tomatoes.

Risotto

This traditional Italian dish has a high UWR rating*, but well worth the effort. Although it is just fancied-up rice, dates seem to find it irresistible. You can serve this as a main dish, or as a side.

What you'll need:

> 1 cup short-grain rice (look for Arborio – it costs a little more but
>   is essential for its creamy texture)
> 1 tablespoon olive oil
> 2 cloves garlic (finely chopped)
> 1 small onion (finely chopped)
> 2 – 3 cups chicken stock
> dash of salt, lots of fresh ground pepper
> 1/4 cup Parmesan cheese

What you'll do:

1. Sauté onion and garlic in olive oil over medium heat until translucent.
2. Add the rice and stir until coated with the onion mixture.
3. Add enough chicken stock to barely cover the rice, reduce the heat to medium-low and cover.
4. Stir often, and add enough stock to keep the rice very moist, almost soupy, but not swimming.
5. Add fresh ground pepper and salt to taste.
6. If using mushrooms, seafood, etc., add in the last few minutes so as not to overcook.
7. Cook until rice is firm, but not crunchy (the Italians call it al dente), and is a nice, creamy texture.
8. Add parmesan, and stir until mixed.
9. Serve with good Italian bread and a nice red wine. You can use it as a side dish or with a salad, as a main.

Tips

1 There are as many varieties of risotto as there are pizza. Experiment to find what ingredients you like best. For example, mushrooms are simple and elegant; adding cooked seafood (mussels, clams and shrimp for example) is decadent.

2 Fresh or dried herbs like rosemary, basil, and/or oregano, is a nice touch.

* In case you missed the other recipes with high UWR ratings, it stands for Upfront Work Required. For our day to day meals, of course, we're looking for almost a zero UWR rating. For meals we're cooking for a new lovely, the higher the UWR rating, the higher up the stairs you'll get.

Veal Marsala

This is a meal that almost everyone who has been to an Italian restaurant has heard of, if not ordered at some time. When you mention to your date that you're making this meal, you'll instantly create a sense of appreciation that you're doing something a little bit special for them. It doesn't matter that this recipe is embarrassingly easy to make; in fact, I'd say it's the easiest in this book.

What you'll need:

> tablespoon of olive oil
> 1/2 pound of veal scallops/scaloppini, about 1/8 in. thick
> 1 cup of Marsala wine
> 1/4 cup of all-purpose flour, seasoned with a couple shakes of salt and pepper
> 1 cup of chicken or vegetable broth

What you'll do:

1. Measure the flour in a measuring cup.
2. Add the salt and pepper. Stir it around to mix.
3. Pour the seasoned flour onto a dinner plate and spread around.
4. Lie the veal flat on the flour to coat it, turn over and coat the other side.
5. Shake off excess flour.
6. Heat oil in skillet.
7. Add veal and sauté about a minute on each side.
8. Once cooked, remove to a platter and cover to keep warm.
9. Add Marsala wine to veal pan. Let boil for a few minutes to thicken.
10. Add the cup of chicken or vegetable stock. and boil for a few more minutes.

What you'll need for the potato side dish:

> small handful of green beans (put these in the microwave to cook when everything else is ready)
> 10 or so small red potatoes
> sprinkle of rosemary
> sprinkle of garlic powder
> 1/2 cup of olive oil

Peter Wright

What you'll do:

1. Wash the potatoes.
2. Place them in a casserole dish.
3. Add the olive oil. Roll the potatoes around to coat in oil.
4. Sprinkle on the rosemary and garlic powder.
5. Make sure there's about 1/8 of an inch of oil in bottom of dish.
6. Place in a preheated oven (350 F) for 1/2 an hour.

Tip

1   Buy the powdered stock – it's so much easier than the cubes. Just add a teaspoon of the stock to a cup of hot water and stir.

STUFF
FOR
DESSERT

Stuff for Dessert

Remember when you were a kid and good ol' Mom made cookies, brownies, a cake or pie? Remember coming home to the smell of cookies baking? Well, there's no reason why you can't do the same for your kids – with a few modifications. I'm all for the aroma, taste and texture of a freshly baked cookie, I just am not that interested in following dessert recipes: putting a dash of nutmeg, a tablespoon of cinnamon, a snitch of salt, a dollop of butter, a smidgen of sugar – shut up! The following products achieve what we're after with the least amount of thinking and preparatory work. For the Dessert section, you'll see I've used the big C/small c designation to indicate whether the dessert is for the goobers (kids) or the gals. As these products all have the instructions on the box, I'm going to mush them all together on the same pages.

Rice Krispie Squares

Even though you can buy those individually wrapped Rice Krispie Squares, it's better to do it this way. Usually the kids help, a little activity together, with a big payout: you get these babies fresh out of the oven. You're supposed to cool them a while to make cutting easier, but who cares. Also, these taste a thousand times better than the ones you buy pre-packaged. This is only a personal observation, but almost double the amount of marshmallows the recipe calls for – they're a little dry otherwise. Also, add some chocolate chips or Smarties for an added treat. I'm not going to write down the recipe – you can find it on the box. (c)

Jell-O

I think Jell-O is one of those forgotten products. I mean, we loved Jell-O as kids. Our kids love Jell-O. And it's so easy to make it's embarrassing. It makes Kraft Macaroni and Cheese look difficult. If you start thinking, "what is this guy, a dolt?! I know about Jell-O," don't forget my goal is to introduce you to and remind you about products that are easy to make and your kids will enjoy eating. My guess, if you're like the majority of dads (myself included up until 7 years ago), you don't think too much about Jell-O, let alone make it. Sometimes if we haven't made something, it leaves our radar screen. I'm just mentioning it because it really is easy to make and the kids love it. (c), and (C) in some very remote cases

Ice cream and chocolate sauce

Sometimes we can forget life's little truths: the earth is round, the XFL was never a good idea, and kids love ice cream – especially with chocolate sauce (or some kind of sauce, i.e., butterscotch). (c)

Ice cream and raspberry sauce

I guess it's also one of life's little truths that women want to feel special, hence the negatory on serving our date the same dessert as the kids (especially on the first date). Mind you, with a couple of changes on the line of scrimmage, we can increase the chance of a good reception. One, upgrade the ice cream (don't be bringing to the table the Family Pak of Igloo's Bulk Ice Creme). Two, put the raspberry sauce in a cream jug and bring to the table. If such a vessel is not available, do the serving in the kitchen. (C)

Sherbet (sorbet)

Ask a few ladies at the grocery store what their favorite flavor of sherbet is. I think the best bet is something at least a little exotic, like raspberry, or peach/mango. It's best to avoid the flavors that have an outside chance of your kids liking. You can also inquire what's the best kind of biscuit/cookie to have with your sherbet. (C)

Cheesecake

Cheesecake is a little tricky. If everyone's comfortable with their weight (rarely a given) and has a sweet tooth (more often a given), cheesecake's a decadent treat. You could make your own from (sort of) scratch using a recipe I saw on a box of Graham Cracker Crumbs, or you can just buy one of the Sara Lee cheesecakes. If you find these a little low-level, ask your supermarket for the frozen cheesecakes (I found a fantastic one in a totally different area that was a New York Cheesecake, so ask). My favorite Sara Lee is the cherry cheesecake, something I know you care deeply about. (C)

Mr. Christie's Chocolate Wafer Log

This is also something that's really easy to make and is really tasty. It doesn't age well, so it's probably just as well you'll eat whatever the kids don't eat at the first sitting. (c)

Cherry, Apple, Blueberry Pie

My kids don't like pie, so I'm a little biased on this. I like pie, women generally like pie and it seems most kids like pie, so that's why it's in here. I know what you're thinking: "pies are best made by grandmothers who grew up in the country, plying their pies at country fairs." You're not thinking that? Oh. I had always shied away from pies because of the supposed artistry in making pie crusts, an art, of course, I wasn't going to participate in. On the other hand, a freshly baked pie with vanilla ice cream is a genuine treat, one that doesn't have to wait for your Mother, Aunt or Grandmother to fulfill. Here's what you can do: buy a frozen pie crust, a tin of pie filling and follow the instructions on the tin. Very simple. (both c's)

Quaker Oatmeal Cookies

These are here only because they were my favorite cookies growing up. They require something this section frowns on: adding ingredients and messing with a mixing bowl. I love the taste, the texture and they remind me of my father, who also loved these cookies. But I can never seem to master the dough transfer from the mixing bowl to the cookie tray. However, if you're in a mixing kind of mood, these cookies are great. One suggestion though: don't buy the mix with the chocolate chips already mixed in, they don't put enough in and somehow alter the mixability, to say nothing of the calibre of the chocolate chips – get some chocolate chips/butterscotch chips or raisins and slap in as many as you want. (c)

Pillsbury

1 Step Cookies (c)

1 Step Brownies (c)

Cinnamon Rolls (c)

Chips Ahoy recently came out with a cookie you can warm up in the microwave oven. On the surface, this sounds like a *Cook Like A Mother!* product – Quick in, Quick Out. But, unfortunately, it's not. They don't stay in the microwave long enough to generate any kind of home cooking aroma, and if they do stay in there long enough, you'd burn the bejesus out of any impatient tongue around the house. The margin for error with the Chips Ahoy cookie is too high: put the cookie in long enough for an aroma of baking cookies in the house and you burn your tongue, a couple of seconds too few and it's just a crappy soft cookie. This is just my opinion, bear in mind. On the other hand, these Pillsbury 1 Step Cookies are perfect because they allow for the complete experience: the aroma, the freshly baked cookies – without having to spend the time with the cookie mix. They're even better, again, in my opinion, than the cookies that come in one of those tubes that you peel back and slice. Who needs to peel and slice when you can just transfer the ragging things from the container to the cookie tray.

The 1 Step Brownies are easy and tasty too, for a change or for those very rare people who either don't like cookies or prefer brownies.

The Cinnamon Rolls are nice and gooey, perfect for a leisurely Saturday or Sunday morning.

Fresh Fruit Salad

My kids aren't big on fruit salad. They'll eat bananas and apples, strawberries and grapes – separately. They eat enough of them that I don't have to spend the time to prepare a fruit salad. For dinner dates, though, fresh fruit salad can't be beat – especially if you use some (relatively) exotic fruits: kiwis and mangos, along with the traditional bananas, grapes, strawberries, oranges, and pink grapefruits. All you have to do is cut the oranges, kiwis, mangos, grapefruit and apples into 1/2 inch cubes, slice the bananas into slices, and throw them all into a salad bowl. Keep the juice from everything for use in the salad and add a cup or so of orange juice.

This fresh fruit thing is very similar to Minestrone soup: there's a terrific amount of Upfront Work Required. It's also very similar in another sense: don't even think of offering a can of fruit salad to your lovely lady friend on your first, second, third . . .date. Frankly, I'm not even sure you can offer it even when you're married – but, hey, you know her better than I do. (both c's)

Bowl of fresh berries with cream

If you can find some fresh blueberries, raspberries or strawberries, you can create a terrific dessert that even the most diet-conscious woman will love. All you have to do is wash the fruit, heave them into a bowl, sprinkle on the fruit a little bit of white sugar (so little you can barely, if at all, see it), take it to the table with a creamer filled with table cream. If this dessert doesn't generate a throaty "mmmmmmmmmm," when she takes the first bite of cream-covered fruit, seriously, you've got the wrong gal. (Mainly Big C)

Nestlé Frothé Dessert Coffees

You know how tricky it is to talk with someone you really want to talk with but you're busy doing something you don't want to screw up? So you kind of sound far less mentally agile than you'd like to? Well, let's make things a little easier for ourselves. Nestlé's Frothé Dessert Coffees require no brains and even less attention, which is a good thing, so you can concentrate on what you're doing – or want to do.

STUFF
TO CLEAN
IT UP
WITH

We're after the easiest and the best: the easiest way to get a job done, the fastest and the best way of doing it. We're after the cleaning tools that make us, the real life Tim the Tool Man, happy. If we could turbo-boost the vacuum and have it operate by robot or virtually from our work computer, great. If there were a way of cleaning the bathroom floor by opening the door a crack, throwing in a cleansing cluster bomb and slamming the door shut, we'd buy it. Or if they could invent a "smart cleaner," along the lines of "smart bombs," that knew where the evil germs were hiding without us having to provide the ground support. That would be the guy's way of cleaning. If there were a way to incorporate a Vulcan mind meld to clean dishes, we'd find it and use it to death.

Unfortunately, the devices I've found worth telling you about fall considerably short of this wishful thinking. On the other hand, these products and approaches are available NOW, are reasonably affordable and give you the precious thing you deserve: time with your children. We know by now the *Cook Like A Mother!* Cooking Credo: Make it tasty, make it fast, clean it quick. The Clean Like a Pro! Cleaning Credo: Do it quick, get it done, get back outside. Every single one of the products I recommend offers a time or step-saving component. This chapter will outline the Stuff that will help you clean up the kitchen, the bathroom, and everywhere you find cobwebs and dust.

Best Cleaning Approach

Of course, even Pentagon-approved cleaning products will not win the war against dirt if you never go into battle with them. One of the things that really differentiates us guys from (most) women is that we don't hear the dirt battle cry to clean as early as they do. It's not really dirty, as far as we're concerned, if it's not visibly dirty. I have to admit I don't have the answer to that dilemma. I'm still of the wait-until-you-can-see-the-color-of-the-dirt mindset, unfortunately. So, in my never-ending quest to be your info provider, I'm about to deviate for the first time in this book: I'm going to propose something I personally don't do. Everything so far in *Cook Like A Mother!* dealt with cooking and cooking-related products or approaches I personally have found useful, but this is one that sounds useful. We'll call it the Practice Day/Game Day approach to cleaning.

The Practice Day/Game Day approach makes best use of something guys can do without any effort whatsoever: organize a practice or game. We can organize a game of touch football every single Sunday at 1:30 p.m. and engineer the attendance of 30 participants, week after week; we can organize a game of golf and coordinate 3 other guys; we can facilitate tennis and squash matches – whatever, without any effort at all. We know our golf game is, say, Sunday morning really early. We know our kid's soccer practice is Thursday night at 6:30 p.m. We know the kid's soccer game is Monday at 7:00 p.m. If we're coaches, we can organize the kids' practices, make the plays, get to the games prepared, and so on and so on. If we're single, we know that every single Thursday, Friday and Saturday we're meeting our friends at Barney's Puck and Ball Joint. We also know we'll clean once a week on the weekend, and we'll try to make sure it happens Saturday morning – unless, of course, something better comes up. In which case, we'll do it Sunday morning, maybe after golf. Or before the football games. Or during halftime. Or maybe after the kids go to bed, well, before Monday Night Football ... .

There's nothing wrong with a casual approach to cleaning – as long as you want to stay single. If you want to stay married (something of which I can only speak academically) or you want to be prepared, here's *The Practice Day/Game Day* approach to cleaning:

Simply, look at your schedule and break down the cleaning requirements, time-wise, the same way you would for games and practices. I'm not going to include Saturday and Sunday because at least one of these days is traditionally a cleaning day, so it's up to you to choose a day to spend 2 hours to clean. My goal with this schedule is to suggest that weekend cleaning time can be minimized by some scheduled cleaning activities throughout the week. And what does this allow? You guessed it, a quicker return to the things we want to be doing. Let's say these are the activities you have to do:

Dusting . . . . How many rooms
Vacuum . . . . How many rooms
Bathrooms. . . . . How many
Kitchen. . . . . Floor, microwave, counters
Laundry . . . . Lights, Darks
Mirrors . . . . How Many
Floors . . . . How Many

Garbage . . . . How many pails/what day is pick up (this garbage thing seems like a no-brainer: You just wait until the pails are full and take it out. The key deterrent to this approach is the lovely odor garbage develops, so this scheduled version precludes you having to be told to take out the stinky garbage if you're married, or your girlfriend comes over and tells you your place stinks, or some variation on the smell theme).

Consider this schedule:

	Monday	Tuesday	Wednesday	Thursday	Friday
6:00	Dinner	Dinner	Dinner	Dinner	Dinner
6:30	Wash bath. Flr.		Soccer Practice		
7:00	Soccer Game	Run/gym	Laundry – lights		Run
8:00			Tennis Ladder		Tennis Ladder
9:00		Vacuum Bdrm.	Wash kit. floor		
9:30	Mirrors			Bar Stool	Bar Stool
10:00	Clean kit. Sink	Clean kit. Sink	Clean kit.		

Keep in mind, when I refer to washing bathroom floor on Monday (especially with the WetJet Swiffer, but more on that in a moment), I'm talking about a 5 minute exercise. When I refer to mirrors, it's a 5 minute thing. So, this scheduling thing looks like a huge time undertaking, but it's not. Either way, I know this is asking a lot. It is probably one of those things that on paper seems like a super idea. I'm not the best with schedules, so I feel a little hypocritical even suggesting one. But, in all fairness, this might be the best way of doing things. I guess what I'm saying is if we attach the same level of commitment and discipline that we attach to games and practices to cleaning, we might not be criticized so often for our (I'll say it again) casual approach to cleaning.

That's all I'm going to say on the schedule subject. It might serve some people really well. At any rate, regardless of WHEN you actually get around to cleaning, these are some products that will make your work a little easier.

Best Cleaning Products – Household

Lysol Antibacterial
Wipes ... Anyone who's had children knows these are merely diaper wipes renamed and an antibacterial ingredient added. But they follow perfectly the *Cook Like A Mother!* cleaning mantra: Do it quick, get it done, get back outside. They're so fast it's as though they come out of a holster, they smell nice, and they fit nicely into the garbage when you're done with them.

Lysol Antibacterial
Spray Cleaner ... No, I don't hold shares in Reckitt Benckiser, the makers of Lysol, but this spray does everything from kitchen counters to bathroom sinks. It even serves as a wall-cleaning spray. I like it because it cleans with the least amount of work, let's face it. There are other cleaners you might as well leave the nozzle closed for how effective they are.

Supertek's MicroFiber
Cleaning Cloths ... These cloths are amazing if you want to use less cleanser when you're cleaning, something of value if you or your kids have allergies. You just wet them and they somehow clean extremely well.

Tide
Rapid Tablets ... Anything that saves time and does a great job has my vote. It doesn't seem very significant, time-wise – the time it takes to scoop out detergent, measure it, put some back, add some, pour it into the washer – but it is. Opening the little packages of Tide takes a second and a half if you're leisurely, then chuck them in and it's done. Also, the clothes smell nice, something the kids like. No, that's not true; my boys never mention it.

Dishwasher Tablets ... Anything in the tablet form is worth a few extra pennies. Doesn't really matter which ones you use.

Best Cleaning Devices

Dishwasher ... Top of the list, without any debate, is the dishwasher, even if you live in an apartment. I cannot even begin to fathom doing the ragging dishes by hand. I bought mine second hand at a reputable (I know, just jinxed the thing) second hand appliance store for $250. It has been a God-send ever since. When you're recently separated you'll go through a number of dark moments, which seem to occur when you find yourself doing things you didn't really do before – like cleaning the base of the toilet, or washing the dishes by hand. If investing in a dishwasher can stave off just one dark moment, it's worth the equivalent of 2.5 hours in therapy. If you're leaving Mom's house for college or your first job, buy a dishwasher before you do almost anything else, like a car, for example – your date would rather take a taxi than help you wash the dishes. On the other hand, loading a dishwasher together after you've cooked a meal is almost a guarantee for . . .

Wetjet Swiffer ... Okay. Brace yourself for what might be the best thing that's ever happened to you – in that very finite part of your life as cleaner. I don't know about you, but I hate cleaning the floors: trekking through the house with a pail of hot water and cleanser, dripping all over the place, having the mop go back and forth between the pail and the floor, spilling a little on your feet, pouring the water into the sink, rinsing out the sink.
I hate it. Let's get serious. I'll admit my disdain for the pail and mop show impedes, shall we say, the frequency of usage. On the other hand, who wants to be tracking through tomato sauce in the kitchen and urine in the bathroom on a daily basis? For us get-in-quick, get-out-just-as-quick set, this Wetjet Swiffer is the best product imaginable.

For the uninitiated, the Wetjet is a product extension of the Swiffer, a dust collector that actually attracts dust to

 Peter Wright

it, and once you're done, you chuck it (the cloth) out. Similarly, with the Wetjet, it's as though you took a Swiffer and attached a squirting device on the front to spurt out and soften up the pancake mix you spilt yesterday. And once you've accumulated enough substances we won't delve into here again, you throw the cleaning pad out. I thought cleaning every Saturday or Sunday couldn't be that bad. "Yeah, I'll just avoid throwing the football around with the kids, playing golf, going for a bike ride, and spend the day cleaning." Uh-huh. However, I don't want to invite the diseases and bad attitudes that a casual approach to household hygiene can cause. So, slap one of these babies in your hand, walk over to the offending floor, spurt as you go, do a few wipes, then put the thing away until next time. It's done in less time than you can locate the bucket and mop.

It's one thing to live alone primarily – with your children whenever you have them, but it's too depressing to live like we did back in our younger days when everything in the kitchen and bathroom was a science project. We're too old for that. The reassuring thing, frankly, is that there are products that can actually do the things we hate doing, and this brings with it a certain perverse thrill to doing it. So, I guess the entire Wetjet Swiffer thing is really a morale booster as well as a floor-cleaning device. Either way, get it; I can assure you it'll be one of the best investments you can make.

Swiffer   ... I realized it would be remiss to mention the Wetjet Swiffer without explaining the value of its ancestor, the Swiffer. If you have any type of flooring aside from carpeting, this is the easiest and fastest way of keeping things looking clean. I must confess it doesn't pick up drops of spaghetti sauce that have become hermetically attached to your floor – the Wetjet has that covered, but if it's just dust and other fine (not quality) particles, the Swiffer's great. It's also great because kids around the age of 10 think they're awesome, so you'll get relief until the novelty wears out.

T-Fal Ultraglide Iron   ... Now that you've done the laundry, everything's nice, clean and smells like Spring ... and wrinkled as a madman. I know what you're thinking – no one will notice it hasn't been ironed, people will think it looks good. Trouble is, they will and they won't. Looks like someone who doesn't mind walking around in wrinkled clothing. So, you drag out the iron you've had since university and spend the next half hour leaving black marks all over your shirt. Nope.

I always thought an iron was an iron, too. It never dawned on me that ironing could be quicker, easier and faster – until I got an iron that had a Teflon coating. It does to ironing, of course, what it does to cooking: speeds things up amazingly. If I can save 3 minutes a shirt, I'm happy. It also has an auto turn-off feature that eliminates sitting in a meeting and suddenly blanching at the thought you may have left your iron plugged in.

Ironing Board   ... The ironing board is to ironing what the cookie tray is to making cookies: you can't do either job well without these products. Just buy the better cover – they're thicker and last longer.

STUFF
WORTH
KNOWING

Eating's pretty easy to do, no real training involved. Our parents fed us when we were too young to do it for ourselves and with luck we've been doing it ever since. Some of us are really good at it, but no point getting into that. When it comes to handling food and preparing what we eat, however, turns out there is stuff worth knowing. Stuff that guys either weren't told about when we were young or we didn't care about. Stuff that could actually make us – and those we love – ill. These are also the things we should know if it becomes evident people are getting the "24 hour flu" quite frequently – as in, after you cook dinner.

Apparently, there is growing evidence that this 24-hour flu is quite often not the flu at all, but a case of food poisoning from improper food handling. In fact, recent research found that there is more fecal matter in our kitchen sinks than in bathroom toilets (our, as in North American, not our, as in guys). I don't know about you, but this doesn't sit well with me. Could, ah, this situation be helped with the occasional hand washing? Which leads me into this chapter on things that guys aren't really known for – hygiene.

I'm the first to admit that until I was the one responsible for cooking and cleaning for the two most cherished things in my life, my two boys, I would never have been confused for the Personal Hygiene Of the Year Spokesperson. When I realized that the food I'm preparing with my very hands and the utensils in them will end up in the mouths of people I love, I became far more attentive to what my hands had done before beginning to make dinner. Don't get me wrong, most people look like they're hygienic, I mean they wear clean clothes, have clean hair, clean fingernails, shiny shoes. But, as our trusty fecal research attests, our hygiene-based decisions might not be the best. Case in point, what's the one thing that could eliminate up to 50% of all cases of food borne illnesses and significantly reduce incidences of the common cold and flu? Think it's something highly technical or scientific? Nope. Washing your hands before, during and after handling food is the number one trick for avoiding the nasties. But sometimes, we try to evaluate the risk by replaying in our head what we've been doing before starting to make dinner. ("What was I just doing? Playing touch football with the kids and their friends. Hmmmmmm. Well, we just got out of the pool, and that's got to be clean, and we played on a newly sodded field, so that really hasn't had time to attract too much dirt, and we're late for the movie, so my hands are fine.") Small thing, BIG risk.

Peter Wright

Speaking of big risk, you know the feeling you get when you can't remember if your chainsaw or lawnmower takes a 50 to 1 gas oil mixture or a 25 to 1? You know the feeling you get when you're trying to decide whether to use synthetic oil or platinum plugs in your new car? Or that queasy feeling we get when we're told the car-wash mittens we've been using actually grind dirt into the paint? Or when you accidentally put your car into drive as you're coasting backwards? This feeling of fear over possible damage to our cars, power tools or sporting goods is a fear most guys are familiar with. It's peculiar, then, that we don't experience the same fears when it comes to eating something from the fridge that, unbeknownst to us, has become a biological warfare case study.

It's a sad truth (well, maybe not sad, but it's true) that while we were helping dad change the spark plugs in the outboard, marvelling at how much better it runs with clean or new plugs, our sisters were learning why you can't eat chicken after it's been in the fridge for a month. She was also learning why you shouldn't leave mayonnaise on the counter for long on a hot day. And, for that matter, she was learning why you shouldn't leave an opened can of Chef Boy R Dee in the fridge for 2 weeks and then eat it.

I just found something out that really annoyed me, and it relates to something I've been doing since the very first time I made meat spaghetti sauce while attending college. For twenty-some odd years, whenever I browned ground beef, I've been adding a little oil, putting in the meat and turning the element on. So NOW I hear that you're supposed to add the oil, margarine or butter – whatever – and turn it on, wait until the pan is up to temperature and THEN add the meat. Why? Because if you do it the way I've been doing it, the oil, butter, whatever, gets absorbed into the meat. Whereas, if you heat the oil up before adding the meat, less of it is absorbed into your food – and we all know that's a good thing. But how in the name of all that's ovenly are we supposed to know this??? (Turns out, once again, that women seem to know this fact, as a friend of mine's wife almost snorted with derision when I mentioned my discovery – 'course, she snorts at most things). So, I've been unknowingly making myself a bigger size because of this approach. And how did I find out about this little known fact? I saw a commercial about a T-Fal skillet that has a red dot in the middle of the pan that changes color when it's up to the healthiest cooking temperature.

But enough of that, let's move on to other areas of Stuff Worth Knowing, such as cleaning. What's the point of cleaning off the kitchen counter – you're just going to use it tomorrow, right? And why bother putting dinner leftovers in the fridge – it can wait until the football game's over (even though they're just tossing the coin). Sarcasm is supposed to be a lower form of humor, but it's fun. So, at risk of stating the obvious, there are a number of key things you must do in the kitchen to maintain health, and here are some of them:

Best 1st Line of Defense: Wash your hands with hot, soapy water for 30 seconds before and after handling food. Doing so could eliminate up to 50% of all cases of food borne illnesses and significantly reduce incidences of the common cold and flu, believe it or not. Frankly, it's a habit you just have to get into. The best way of getting into the habit is to imagine a restaurant that serves pasta with their unwashed hands, or adds ingredients by hand after sneezing. That's gross, isn't it? So, you have to keep an effective image in your mind that forces you to do something you might not be doing right now – especially if you're eating alone. It's too difficult a habit to break if you ever have company and she sees you starting to make dinner without washing your hands first. Creates a bad first impression, shall we say.

Best 1st Line of Defense 2: Wash each utensil, knife, serving spoon, plate – everything that comes into contact with food BEFORE it comes into contact with other food. This may seem a little neurotic until you realize cross-contamination is one of the best ways to get e-coli, a weigh-loss program that's extremely violent and extremely worth avoiding.

Barbecuers Beware: It may be easier and quicker to put those beautifully done steaks back onto the plate you carried them out on, but DON'T. This simple mistake is made all summer long with predictable results: people get upset stomachs and feel ill for a day or so. They mistakenly think it's the 24-hour flu, but, once again, it's a case of being exposed to bacteria that proper cooking eliminates.

Peter Wright

Proper fridge temperature: 40° F. Stop wondering why your milk tastes funny – turn the temperature down!

Proper fridge management:
- Don't store milk or eggs on the door.
- Discard deli meats after 5 days.
- Discard cooked pasta and pizza after 3 – 5 days.
- Cooked rice should be punted after 5 days.

Leftover Law: It's easy to forget to put leftovers from dinner parties away into the fridge immediately, because there's so much going on. The fact is you should refrigerate hot foods as soon as possible – within two hours after cooking. If it's been standing out for more than two hours, pitch it. Don't bother trying to taste-test it, either. Even a small amount of contaminated food can cause illness. Date leftovers so they can be used within a safe time. Generally, they remain safe when refrigerated for three to five days. "If in doubt, throw it out." Reheat leftovers to at least 165° F. Very important. Bacteria can be eliminated by proper cooking and reheating – an easy way to stay out of the bathroom.

The Cutting Board: The best way to clean a cutting board is in the dishwasher. If you're still making dinner, use soap and hot water. This is especially important if you've just been cutting poultry, seafood or raw meat. Wiping with a damp cloth will not remove bacteria, so if you cut vegetables on the cutting board you've just used for, say, poultry, even if you wiped with a clean, wet cloth, don't be too surprised that people have stomach aches after they eat your dinner. If you don't have a dishwasher, sanitize it with a mild bleach solution after using soap and hot water.

Hamburger Help: E-coli has such an ugly ring to it, and an even uglier reality. Think of ground beef as e-coli's primary means of transportation, and the only way to make sure the bus doesn't stop at your home is to ensure your burgers are properly cooked. Regardless of how you like your burgers done, the safest way to cook them is until they are no longer red in the center and the juices run clear. Better yet, use a meat thermometer and cook to 160° F. And don't even think of giving a child a rare burger. Undercooked hamburgers cause more children to be ill every summer than swimming in Lake Erie. If you do not have a meat thermometer, don't eat ground beef patties that are still pink in the middle. Make life easier for yourself by stabbing the sucker with a meat thermometer and make sure it gets up to 160° F.

Do the Dishes! The best way to do the dishes, from a bacteria-prevention standpoint, is the either do them in a dishwasher, or, if you don't have one yet, put them into hot water, wash them immediately (after immersion), rinse, and let them air dry. If you put dishes in the sink, let them soak for a couple of hours and then do them, you've unwittingly created dish soup, where the food has contributed to the main ingredient: bacteria. Also, the problem with hand towels is that bacteria get spread around, joyously.

Raw poultry, fish or meat handling: Let's say you're making dinner; you take the chicken breasts out of the package, and put them in the dish for marinating. Then what? Wash your hands immediately with soap and warm water for 20 seconds. If you have a cut, best to wear rubber gloves.

Poultry, fish or meat defrosting: It's good to know that smaller items will defrost more evenly than larger ones. Keep that in mind when packaging chicken breasts and hamburger, as detailed in the section, Stuff to Make it With. You should cook with these thawed meats immediately after thawing. Incidentally, don't thaw poultry, meat and fish on the counter; bacteria get very amorous at room temperature and multiply too quickly.

Fruits and Vegetables:

- Don't refrigerate tomatoes, bananas, potatoes, onions.
- Do refrigerate plums, peaches only after they've ripened and sweetened on your counter.
- Do refrigerate cantaloupes, honeydew and other melons unless you plan to eat them within a few days.
- Don't eat potatoes with "eyes" as they are roots that contain a natural chemical that helps the suckers grow but can actually make you (or your kids) sick.
- Don't eat tomatoes that "leak" under any circumstances. The leakage says there's bacteria present that can cause stomach upset and worse. (Read: bathroom trip).

STUFF
YOUR
KIDS
CAN DO

Ever been out at the mall, a restaurant or a kids' ballgame and hear a parent hollering at their kid "WHY DID YOU DO THAT?! WHY!" Then, the kid gets yanked, smacked and hauled off to some unseen fate or gets the cold-shoulder psychological punishment. It could be, of course, the kid did something horrendous and deserved to be "corrected." A lot of other times, however, kids get in grief for acting exactly as they should be acting for their age. It turns out, a fair amount of child abuse stems from the parent not knowing what to expect from children at their different stages of development. Instead of recognizing the child's behavior as completely normal, even healthy, the parent reacts angrily, questioningly.

It doesn't do the child's self-esteem any good being reamed out for normal behavior. This has terrific relevance when it comes to chores. It's really important to us to have a clear understanding of what the child is capable of doing. We know for sure they want to please us (for the most part) and they will try their best at what we ask them. It's monumentally important, then, that we choose chores that are within their capabilities in order to build their self-esteem. We can't be asking an 8 year old to dust the living room, the one with your parent's china.

On the other hand, it's difficult for many parents to institute chores and responsibilities because they're working long hours and don't feel right walking in the door and issuing orders. Indeed, many parents feel guilt at having to work as much as they do, so they resort to being lenient – mainly because it's easier. Choosing and assigning chores, doing a schedule and sticking to it is almost like work – it takes time and thought. The key thing is you have to be firm, it's not one of those "if you feel like it or have the time, please empty the dishwasher." Like all subordinates, they'll try to argue, plead and connive their way out of doing the chores. It's easier, sometimes, just to say " 'eff it, I'll do it myself." But chores are not simply something the kids can do to help you out – although that's the selfish motivation.

There is considerable research that claims two key benefits to kids doing chores:

1. Chores make the kids feel like a responsible, contributing member of the family.
2. Chores, or rather, a clean/tidy house, can help the kids do better in school and life. Why? Because doing chores regularly help the kids learn time-management skills (you can't play baseball or that GD video game until your room is clean).

But you may say, "sure, the kids should be doing chores, but we're so busy or I see them so infrequently, I don't want to be harping at them to do chores." Unfortunately, this perpetuates the notion that Dads are just around for the fun, not the parenting. So, we're going to do this like we did the cleaning schedule. Why? Mainly because cleaning sucks, no one likes to do it, and schedules are one of those unarguable things, "Well, Fiona, you have to do the dishes tonight because it's on the schedule."

When it comes to things like chores and allowance, I always thought I was doing the right thing, helping mold the correct, life-lesson reactions in my kids. Like, making their allowances tied to household chores. For me, this made terrific sense, thinking that I'm just training or preparing them for the time when they begin working. It shouldn't be a novelty for them if they've been working for money for years, or so I thought. I also thought I should make unpleasant chores or activities more acceptable by rewarding them for getting the chores done, as in, "we'll go to McDonald's if you put your toys away NOW."

Unfortunately, it turns out I'm wrong on both counts – and I hate that. Turns out, "experts" now feel that if you decide to give your child an allowance, it shouldn't be tied to chores. This is not to say you shouldn't enlist the child's help to assist in household chores, rather, the experts are not convinced you should pay the kids for the chores. Why? Because when the child's need for money changes, say they get a real job when they're a teen or Aunt Chainsmoker left a tidy sum in her will that the kid has some miraculous access to the interest payments, in their mind they don't have to do the chores anymore because they don't need the money. And let's see you try to convince them they now can do the same chores for free. Noooo, it's best to tell them the chores have to be done as part of a well-oiled household machine, supplied by them, a very significant cog.

Regarding "rewards," I found out recently that using rewards, say treats or stickers, for certain behavior, accomplishments, attitudes, etc., can have a negative effect. It turns out that the use of these incentives can actually make a kid enjoy the activity, sport, etc., even less than they did BEFORE you started amusing yourself with the ragging little stickers. I feel especially bad about this because all this time I thought I was being Head Coach of the Year of our local Atom football team. I've been giving out stickers for Best Tackler, Best Blocking Back, First Touchdown, Best Looking Mom (oops, that was a coaches award), etc., after each game. The kids seem to love getting the stickers and I felt like a champ, thinking I'm doing something positive for the kids. Then I read the research that shows that giving kids stickers for something is the best way to get them to dislike doing it! No wonder our enrollment is down! Just kidding. Mind you, maybe this research is done by the same people who first said to stay away from butter, only to tell us almost 10 years later the kind of hydrogenized oil found in most margarines will kill you far faster than any dairy product. Sigh. Then again, all I can do is make you aware of prevailing views; I can't advise you on whether to follow them.

Just to put some bite, as it were, to our chore message, according to the US Department of Education OFFICE OF EDUCATIONAL RESEARCH AND IMPROVEMENT, any household task can become a good learning game and can be fun for toddlers and pre-schoolers. I have a little difficulty thinking pre-schoolers can do much beyond taking their laundry to the laundry room, though. I personally think chores start with any real contribution around 8, but maybe that's just my kids.

What you'll need:

> Jobs around the home that need to get done, such as:
> Carrying out the garbage
> Doing the laundry
> Doing the dishes
> Drying the dishes
> Loading or unloading the dishwasher
> Dusting
> Setting the dinner table

Peter Wright

What you'll do:

1. Explain the job you will first do together. Explain why the family needs the job done. Describe how you will do it and how your child can help.
2. Teach your child new words that belong to each job. "Let's put the placemats on the table, along with the napkins. NOW."
3. Doing laundry together provides many opportunities to learn. Ask your child to help you remember all the clothes that need to be washed. See how many things he/she can name. Socks? T-shirts? Pajamas? Bra? Give me that! Have him/her help you gather all the dirty clothes. Have your child help you make piles of light and dark colors.

Show your child how to measure out the soap (unless, of course, you've read the section on Stuff to Clean it Up With, then you'd be putting detergent tabs in), and have him/her pour the soap into the machine. Let them put the items into the machine, naming them. After the wash is done, have your child sort their own things into piles that are the same (for example, T-shirts, socks).

Home chores can help children learn new words, how to listen and follow directions, how to count, and how to sort.

To assign chores, let's give them some perspective so we don't get all cranky when our 7 year-old steps into the bucket of floor cleaner and spills it all over the floor.

Chore	Key Elements	Key Requirements
Setting the table	Deciding what's necessary	Ability to handle glasses and knives
Dusting	Attention to detail	Ability to direct the spray of furniture polish, handle/move knickknacks
Vacuuming	All parts of the room	Ability to carry something heavy/move furniture, and not knock things over
Cleaning bathroom	Washing sink, toilet, tub	Ability to use cleaner responsibly
Laundry	Sorting, adding detergent	Ability to sort clothes, measure detergent
Floors	Recognize clean	Ability to use mop and bucket or Swiffer

At what ages, then, can children do these chores? It's difficult to use hard and fast rules for an age/chore evaluation. It's probably more productive to go through a little mental check list.

Agility	What it really boils down to is deciding when the child is competent to handle certain physical tasks. If you've ever coached or seen a game of t-ball, soccer or hockey played by 5 year olds, you'd know instantly they're not ready to carry anything sharp or fragile. Some can, but they'd be the exception. Can they aim, with reasonable consistency, one of those spray cans, or do they still get it in the face? If they can't aim, it's too early to dust.
Strength	At what age is a child strong enough to carry the garbage or the vacuum? Hard to say. 9 or 10 if the kid's pretty strong. 11 or 12 might be safer. In both cases, it's important not to assign this task if there's a chance they could drop the garbage down the stairs, requiring a massive clean up, or the vacuum down the stairs, taking out the 2 kids playing Checkers at the bottom of the stairs.
Maturity	Does the child know the consequences of gnawing on a Tide tablet? Are the cleaning supplies still locked? Does the kid still think Windex looks like Gatorade? If they're well past these questions, they can certainly measure laundry and dish detergent. They could certainly clean the windows.

And lastly, let's say you've achieved total buy-in for doing chores. You've managed to get your kids to accept the chores without expecting to be paid and everything's beautiful. So, what's the best way of assigning chores to minimize chore fatigue and eliminate gender bias? Chore Rotation.

Let's say you've got two kids, Billy and Sarah. Here's a schedule you could consider:

Week 1	Monday	Tuesday	Wednesday	Thursday	Friday	Saturday	Sunday
Billy	Dinner table set	Dinner table set	Dinner table set	Dinner table set	Dinner table set	Dinner table set	Dinner table set
Sarah	Table clearing	Table clearing	Table clearing	Table clearing	Table clearing	Table clearing	Table clearing
Billy	Living room tidy			Living room tidy	Call for pizza pizza	Tidy room	Garbage take-out
Sarah	Kitchen floor			Kitchen floor	Clothes to laundry room	Tidy room	
Billy	Load dishwasher		Load dishwasher		Load dishwasher		Load dishwasher
Sarah	Empty dishwasher		Empty dishwasher		Empty dishwasher		Empty dishwasher

Week 2, of course, reverses or rotates chores. I know this appears to be a complex pain in the ass, but it takes about 1 minute to prepare, you can tack it up next to the soccer schedules and it becomes part of your family's life. The best advice on chores: think about what the kids are capable of doing, ask them if they think they're capable of doing them (not do they want to do them), devise a schedule, AND STICK TO IT.

Allowances

Allowances are important. You can name all the same good reasons for giving allowances: helps with number counting, money management, responsibility, helps eliminate the "can you buy me some gum?," etc. In terms of guidelines, you can't say $.50 for 5 year olds, $0.75 for 6 year olds, $1.00 for 7 year olds, and so on. What is appropriate, though, is a combination of your means and what other kids your child hangs around with receive. If most of the other 10 year olds are getting $5.00 a week and you're still giving $2.00, it needs adjustment. Unless, of course, that's all you can afford. Then the kid has to be happy with what he/she gets – and you can explain that: "You have a choice, you can be happy with $2.00 or unhappy with no dollars, it's up to you." That may be a glib way of dealing with it, but sometimes glib beats the 30 minute real explanation of why every family has to set budgets based on income and this is the amount we have allocated to our kids' allowances – then again, if you have the 30 minutes, it's probably better they understand the context and reasoning.

Metric Conversion Chart

When I first started *Cook Like A Mother!*, I had to decide how much information you might want to have. The thrust of *Cook Like A Mother!* is to give you the ability to make decent meals without too much screwing around, so the recipes are pretty basic. For this reason, I decided not to clutter the page with metric conversions. So, here's a handy-dandy conversion chart that lets us seem far smarter than we really are.

Oven temperatures		Volume		Mass Weight	
250°F	120°C	1/4 tsp	1 ml	1 ounce (oz)	28 grams
275°F	140°C	1/2 tsp	2 ml	1 pound (lb)	450 grams
300°F	150°C	1 tsp	5 ml	1 gram (g)	.035 ounces
325°F	160°C	1 tbsp	15 ml	1 kilogram (kg	2.2 pounds
350°F	180°C	1/4 cup	50 ml		
375°F	190°C	1/3 cup	75 ml		
400°F	200°C	1/2 cup	125 ml		
425°F	220°C	2/3 cup	150 ml		
450°F	230°C	3/4 cup	175 ml		
475°F	240°C	1 cup	250 ml		
500°F	260°C				

tsp =   teaspoon = the spoon kids eat cereal or soup with

tbsp =   tablespoon = the spoon we eat cereal or soup with

ACKNOWLEDGEMENTS

There you have it – almost 8 years of cooking and cleaning experiences, lessons and insights. Eight years of ensuring the kids are properly fed, presentably dressed, clean and not living in squalor. There have been times, for sure, that I've wished things were different and that I didn't have to do everything for the most part by myself. It would have been so much easier, as the check-out lady at the local grocery store told me, to just get a girl friend "so I wouldn't have to worry about cooking and cleaning." It was important to me, however, to do everything myself for the simple reason that when I got married again (big assumption), it would be out of want, not need.

It has been indescribably important to me to be part of my kids' growing up. Anyone who has been through a separation or divorce knows how challenging it is to arrive at custody arrangements both parents can support. In the past, the law generally awarded mothers with custody, with very little regard for the father's role in their kids' lives. Finally, though, research is supporting the view that kids deserve to spend equal time with each parent, that each parent's contribution is important to a child's development and well-being. To that end, I'm hoping *Cook Like a Mother!* will remove the obvious deterrent to shared parenting: how can dad have the kids half the time if he can't cook?

Mind you, nothing should replace a father's time with his children, not even divorce. I would not have wanted anything to replace the experiences my kids and I have had over the last 8 years – the laughter, tears, band-aids, burnt chicken, football games, stitches, pneumonia, chicken pox, school plays, homework, projects – in short, everything.

Being able to take care of my kids equally and competently has become a great source of pride for me. I hope the things in this book let you be the dad – single or otherwise – you want to be as well.

On a lighter note, I must thank my mother, Jean Wright, who has demonstrated terrific restraint and tolerance to my never-ending cooking and cleaning questions. I'm eternally grateful to Lorna Robb, who has been extremely supportive and also very patient – about everything, this book included. My sister Karen deserves a special thanks for actually testing the recipes. And, I'd like to thank my nephew Michael, for taking the time to write and send me his recipes and Dave and Julie Read who were also a terrific help by providing editorial help and great suggestions.

Without a doubt, my biggest thanks goes to Karen Petherick of Intuitive Design, who not only is responsible for how my book looks, she's responsible for how it didn't look – full of little errors or inconsistencies I couldn't see. Without her, my first foray into the book publishing world would indeed have looked that way.

A big thanks goes to the following companies for their financial assistance:

Shoppers Drug Mart, Credit Landing, Port Credit, Ontario
Nestlé Canada Frothé Dessert Coffee (Frothy in Canada)
South West Football Association (MFL)
T-Fal Canada

INDEX

toaster oven, 12
Tomato Steak, 78
tomatoes
    adding sugar to, 79
    and bacteria, 107
    peeling, 46
tools
    for kitchens, 11
    and performance, 10
tuna
    Pasta Putanesca, 79
    Tuna Casserole, 51
Tuna Casserole, 51
turkey, ground, 62
turnips, peeling, 60

U
utensils, 17-18
    washing, 104
    whisk, 74

V
Veal Marsala, 82-83
vegetables, 27
    broccoli, 55
    Caesar Salad, 73-74
    cutting, 34, 36
    Dave's Prague Peppers, 64-65
    grilling peppers, 76
    leeks, 60
    peeling tomatoes, 144
    peeling turnips, 60
    potato side dish, 82-83
    storing, 107
W
washing dishes, 106
Wetjet Swiffer, 98-99
whisk, 74
wok, 12
    Take a Wok, Man!, 31-32
    tips on using, 32

Y
Yer Traditional Roast Chicken, 54-55

Z
Ziploc Containers, 20